ENCYCLOPAEDIA OF INDIAN GOVERNMENT: PROGRAMMES AND POLICIES

ENCYCLOPAEDIA
OF
INDIAN GOVERNMENT:
PROGRAMMES AND POLICIES

Vol. 23

Home Affairs and National Security

Edited by

Satish Tiwari

ANMOL PUBLICATIONS PVT. LTD.

NEW DELHI - 110 002 (INDIA)

ANMOL PUBLICATIONS PVT. LTD.
4374/4B, Ansari Road, Daryaganj
New Delhi - 110 002

Encyclopaedia of Indian Government: Programmes and Policies

First Edition, 2000
ISBN 81-261-0515-1 (Set)

PRINTED IN INDIA

Published by J.L. Kumar for Anmol Publications Pvt. Ltd., New Delhi - 110 002 and Printed at Mehra Offset Press, Delhi.

Contents

Preface *vii*

1. Introduction 1
2. Organisation 12
3. Jammu & Kashmir 25
4. North-East 40
5. Union Territories 54
6. National Security 73
7. India's Foreign Affairs 117

Preface

Encyclopaedia of Indian Government: Programmes and Policies contains authoritative information on about fifty departmental policies and their future developmental programmes.

Organised to be completed in 40 volumes, this gigantic work covers Agriculture; Atomic Energy; Chemicals and Fertilizers; Coal; Commerce; Communication; Culture; Defence; Education; Environment and Forests; External Affairs; Finance; Food & Consumer Affairs; Food Processing Industries; Health and Family Welfare; Home Affairs and Internal Security; Human Resources; Industry; Information and Broadcasting; Labour; Law, Justice and Company Affairs; Non-conventional Energy Sources; Ocean Development; Parliamentary Affairs; Personnel, Public Grievances and Pensions; Petroleum and Natural Gas; Planning and Programme Implementation; Planning and Statistics; Posts and Telegraphs; Power; Rural Development; Science and Technology; Social Justice and Empowerment; Space; States Affairs; Steel; Steel and Mines; Sugar and Edible Oils; Surface Transport; Textiles; Tourism; Urban Development; Water Resources; Women and Child development etc.

Based on the information derived from authoritative sources, this work contains authentic facts and figures. I am deeply beholden to all the scholars whose writings are cited or substantially made use of in the present work. I am also thankful to Anmol Publications Pvt. Ltd. for undertaking publication of this encyclopaedia. I am solely responsible for shortcomings in presentation of matter.

Encyclopaedic in nature, this will prove a dependable reference work for scholars and academics besides those appearing for different competitive examinations.

—**Satish Tiwari**

1

Introduction

The internal security situation in India continues to be 'proxy war' unleashed by Pakistan in Jammu & Kashmir, 'insurgence' related problems in some States in the North- East, sporadic violence in by divisive forces and traditional crimes and social tensions. During the last year, several initiative taken by the Government-both in anticipating the problems with a view to preventing them and for containing terrorism-have yielded positive results. The implementation of internal security policies towards strengthening the State Government and overall capability of the Indian States has been accelerated.

Apart from the major task of maintaining the internal security of the country, the responsibilities of the Ministry of Home Affairs cover a wide are of subjects stretching from Central Para- Military Forces to Centre-State Relations, National Integration, Human Right and Rehabilitation of Refuges. Internal security itself has many dimensions, starting with terrorism and militancy in Jammu & Kashmir to separatist insurgency and the threat from demographic changes in the North-East. There are the so-called 'ideological' movements to contend with, namely, Left-Wing extremism in Andhra Pradesh, the Greater Godavari Region and parts of Madhya Pradesh, and the caste-wars spearheaded by private 'senas' in Bihar. Combating cross-border terrorism, countering espionage and generally foiling external conspiracies aimed at destabilizing our border region, keeping up the efficiency and morale of the Central Police Organisations, especially those units combating militancy and terroism on our borders, engaged constant attention of the Ministry throughout the year. Protection of processes and traditions constituted an important element of the activities of the Ministry.

Low and order

The overall low and order situation in the country remained, by and large, satisfactory during the year under report, except for insurgent and militant activities in the North-East and Jammu & Kashmir, Left-wing extremist violence in parts of Andhra Pradesh, Bihar, Madhya Pradesh, Maharashtra and Orissa and caste and ethnic conflicts and communal tensions in certain States. However, fundamentalist mercenaries targeted Hindu families in the Kashmir valley and in Doda. Some incidents targeted against Christians also did take place in Madhya Pradesh, Gujarat and Orissa. Caste wars in Bihar took a considerable toll of lives. At the same time, there was a decline in communal violence and there was no large-scale sectarian flare-up in the country.

Jammu & Kashmir

With an overall improvement in the situation prevailing in the State of Jammu & Kashmir, the drive against militancy has entered a crucial phase. The valley, which was the militants' main base target, is comparatively quit. Since the Lok Sabha and Assembly Elections inn 1996, the law and order situation has progressively improved. However, there has been considerable, if not corresponding, upsurge inn militancy in Jammu region of the State which threatens to spill over to neighbouring States. There has been a significant change in the nature of militancy in the State; foreign mercenaries from across the border now dominate the scene, thereby giving Pakistan a stranglehold over prominent secessionist militant groups which are being used by ISI for bringing in a communal divide, fore, ethnic cleaning and for extending the arc of militancy to Jammuu and beyond. The key, therefore, is to curb and, possible, stop infiltration from across the border. Because of the improving situation, mercenaries become desperate and attacked soft targets in far out villages. These sneak attacks targeted Hindu families in villages like Wandhama, Prankot and Sampnari, mostly in Udhampur and Doda districts.

The four principal of Government's policy vis-a-vis Jammu & Kashmir, being executed by the Union and the State Government, are:—

— Deepening of the democratic process.

— Isolation of the militant and foreign mercenaries from the people.

— Pro-active role within Jammu & Kashmir to neutralise the hostile the hostile designs of militants and foreign mercenaries.

— Galvanising the Development Programmes.

Due to oprationalisation of a carefully action plan to contain, and eventually wipe out militancy in Jammu & Kashmir- which includes curbing infiltration countering militancy inn the hinterland, protection of minorities, tackling the alienation of the border population, enhancing intelligence capabilities and greater functional integration-the ground situation has improved significantly. Trade and economic activities, especially tourism which has traditionally been the back-bone of the valley's economy, have shown sure-signs of revival, with greater number of tourists visiting the State. An unprecedented record of nearly 1.5 lakh pilgrims participating in the Amarnath Yatra was established in 1998.

North-east

The North-east, with its plethora of ethnic groups, each asserting its identity obsessively; its history of isolation fostered by the British; and the perception prevailing amongst its people that concessions can be extracted from the Central Government by taking to the gun, has been a source of worry over the last fifty years. Matters have been exacerbated by large scale migration of population from Bangladesh. The seven states of the North-East have international boundaries with four foreign countries, China, Myanmar, Bangladesh and Bhutan. Though insurgency movement are seen in Nagaland, Assam, Manipur and Tripura, there is a positive signal towards peace and dialogue from this area, as can be evidenced from the state of affairs in Mizoram which is one of the most peaceful states in the country today. A ceasefire between the Security Forces and the main insurgent group, the NSCN (I/M) prevailed for most of the year and a political representative, Shri Swaraj Kaushal, is holding talks with the NSCN on behalf of the Government of India. Despite the ceasefire, kidnaping and extortions by the NSCN (I/M) slightly vitiated the atmosphere.

Assam, which was free from this until 1979, was drawn into the vortex of insurgency beginning with the agitation on foreigners' issue and the subsequent formation of ULFA. This was further aggravated by the Bodo problem and Bodo-Santhal clashes.

The insurgency in Manipur, which was on a low profile in 1950s, assumed an ominous character in the late 1960s. As against that, the insurgency in Nagaland has been a factor to be reckoned with right since independence. In Tripura, it was the large scale influx of Bengali population into the State in the 1960s that sowed the seed of discontent, because the Tripura had become a minority in his own state. The Central Government had taken a number of measures to insurgency in the North-East. These include:—

— Declaration of major insurgent group (such as National Socialistic council of Nagaland, United Liberation Front of Assam, National Democratic Front of Bodoland, Bodo Liberation Tiger, the 5 Meitei Extremist Group, All Tripura Tiger Force and National Liberation Front of Tripura) as 'Unlawful Associations' under the Unlawful Activities (Prevention) Act, 1967.

— Deployment of units of Central Para Military Forces as will as Army in the insurgency- affected States.

— Reimbursement of security related expenditure of insurgency-affected States in the North-East.

— Construction of border roads and border fencing on Indo-Bangladesh border to check infiltration.

— Grants totaling Rs.144.30 crores by the Tenth Finance Commission to the North-Eastern States for Police Housing, Police Telecommunications, construction of Police Stations/Outposts, repair and renovation of Jails, etc.

— Upgradation of arms and ammunition, vehicles, communication and other equipment in the North-Eastern States.

— Mutual discussion and consultation with the Government of Bangladesh, Myanmar and Bhutan on security matters of mutual concern.

— A package of initiatives, amounting to Rs.6133 crores for the development of the North-East now stand at Rs.7865 crores following inclusion of certain additional schemes in the package (the package includes schemes for development of the North-East in priority sectors like Health, Education, Transport, Food control's.

Punjab militancy

The remnant of the Punjab militancy is largely sustained by terrorists based in Pakistan and some other countries and their mentor, the Pak ISI. Security Forces have been able to arrest some terrorists and recover large quantities of explosives, including RDX. Visible improvement in the situation notwithstanding, Punjab remains vulnerable to sporadic terrorist action by the remaining militants who are under pressure from the Pak ISI to revive the separatist movement. Vigilance, therefore, is the key to preserving peace in Punjab.

As part of the strategy devised by the Government for effective policing of the western border with Pakistan and for curbing infiltration/exfiltration of mercenaries/ militants/drug-traffickers from across the border and for effectively combating transborder terrorism, fencing/food lighting of the Indo-Pak border in the States of Punjab and Rajasthan has been taken up from 1988 onwords. A total length of 451 Kms. of fencing and 465 Kms. of floodlighting in the entire Punjab sector, with the exception of some gaps in riverine areas was completed in 1993.

In the Rajasthan sector, a stretch of 865 Kms. has been fenced/floodlit upto December 31, 1997 and the work of fencing/ flood lighting in the remaining 167.60 Kms. in Rajasthan and 10 Kms. of Luni river basin in the Rann of Kutch adjoining Rajasthan sector is under execution and is likely to be completed by December 31,1999. The sealing of the Jammu International Border by fencing/lighting and an intruder alarm system along the border has also been planned and the work will be taken up at an appropriate time.

Left-wing extremism

Left-wing extremism continues to remain a disruptive force in some part of the country, especially Andhra Pradesh, Bihar, Madhya Pradesh, Maharashtra and Orissa.

Andhra Pradesh and Bihar are the major theatres of Left-wing extremist activities, accounting for most of the incident and casualties. Though in terms of the number of incident, Left-wing extremist violence has shown a downward trend since 1996, the incident of violence continues to remain high as reflected in the number of casualties.

The Union Home Ministry took the initiative of convening a meeting of the Chief Ministers of Andhra Pradesh, Madhya Pradesh, Maharashtra and Orissa to review Left-wing extremist activities and the action being taken by the concerned States. As a result of the follow up action taken on the decisions arrived at in this meeting, the Ministry set up a Coordination Centre headed by the Union Home Secretary with the Chief Secretaries and Directors General of Police of these four States as its members. Subsequently, representative of the Government of Bihar were included in it. The states have been advised to prepare action plans for the integrated development of the affected areas and send these to the Ministry of Home Affairs, to be taken up with the planning Commission for earmarking separate funds for the purpose. The requests for upgradation of equipment and weaponry and other security related needs of the Police Forces are being handed on priority basis.

Cast and communal violence

Caste rivalries have socio-economic dimension to them but something spill over into caste violence. Apart from Bihar, there were no major incident of caste violence in the rest of the country. Major causative factors behind caste related incidents/tensions continue to be land disputes, atrocities against Scheduled Castes, molestation of Dalit women, prevention of Harijans from participating in local religious festivals, damage to/ desecration of statues of OBC/Dalit and other leaders by rival caste groups, controversies over naming/renaming of place and institutions, etc. The Ministry of Home Affairs has been interacting with the State Governments on a regular basis to help create adequate awareness among the States of the dimension of internal security problems and foster greater coordination of efforts among the Central and State Governments.

On the Communal front, there has been a marked decline in communal violence during the year 1998 as compared to the previous year. The year witnessed 626 incidents claiming 207 lives and 2065 injuries as compared to 725 incidents resulting in the death of 264 persons and injuries to 2503 as in the previous year.

About 90% of the communal incidents were reported from the States of Uttar Pradesh, Bihar, Madhya Pradesh, Gujarat, Maharashtra, Rajasthan, Delhi, West Bengal, Karnataka and Tamil Nadu. Except for Karnataka, Maharashtra and Rajasthan, which registered slight upswing in communal incidents, all other States reported a declining trend. However, Andhra Pradesh witnessed more deaths in 1998 as compared to previous year due to a major riot in Hyderabad.

Although the communal violence has been on the decline since 1993, the communal divide widened due aggressive postures adopted by both Hindu and Muslim fundamentalist organisations. Clearly, the threshold of communal disturbances, particularly on account of manifold increase in activities of organisations like Al-Umma, TMMK, MIM, NDF, etc. In the year 1998, there were 84 incident as against 30 incident during the corresponding period of 1997. Some of these cases were crime oriented and it was a coincidence that the victims were Christians. In a few cases the attack were deliberate and dastardly, as the burning alive of Graham Stewart Staines and his two sons in Orissa would go to show.

Certain religious organizations accused Christian missionaries of proselytisation activities, but this could in no way justify such 'retaliation'. Some attacks on Christians and their institutions in Gujarat and Orissa hogged the headlines in the national dailies and invited sharp criticism of the States Governments in taking adequate preventive action. The Government has shown its determination to put down such incident with a firm hand.

'Public order' and 'Police' being State subjects, it for the concerned it is or the concerned State Governments to devise various methods and take concrete steps to improve the law and order situation in the States. The Constitution, however, places a duty on the Central Government to protect every States not only against external aggression but also from internal disturbance and to ensure that the Government in every State is carried out in accordance with the provisions of the Constitution. In the Ministry of Home Affairs, action is taken to facilitate coordination of anti-terrorist operations of different States and to improve the flow of information, useful for control of their activities, among the States.

Further, help is being provided to the State Government in terms of financial assistance for modernisation of Police, supply of improved weapons, deployment of Para Military Force, etc. In certain special circumstances, financial assistance has been provided to some of the affected States over and above the on-going allocations for modernisation of police and the supply of weapons.

Policy initiatives/responses

Several other policy initiatives were taken to help serve the cause of peace and order, harmony and social progress in the country, some of the important once being:—

— reconstitution of the Inter-State Council in October 1998 and holding of the Fifth meeting of the Council on January 22,1999;

— introduction of the Uttar Pradesh Reorganisation Bill, 1998, the Bihar Reorganisation Bill, 1998 and the Madhya Pradesh Reorganisation Bill, 1998 in the Lok Sabha in December, 1998;

— grants-in-aid to voluntary agencies with a view to promoting communal harmony, achieving national integration and strengthening bonds of unity and brotherhood in the country;

— circulation of guidelines to all States for promotion of communal harmony and protection of the minority communities;

— introduction of PIO (Persons of Indian Origin) Card scheme extending the Card-holders from the requirement of visa and extending to them other benefits in the economic, educational, financial and cultural fields;

— introduction of the Explosive Substances (Amendment) Bill with a view to putting highly lethal explosive such as RDX, PETN, HMX and similar other explosives under 'Special Category Explosive Substances' and providing for enhancement of the maximum punishment for offences committed with such explosive substances;

— proposal for introduction of a Bill for amendment of the Indian Penal Code providing for capital punishment for rape;

— emphasis on protection on human right of all people in the country; and

— impetus to the scheme of write fencing and flood-lighting of borders to prevent cross border terrorism and smuggling of arms and drugs.

2

Organisation

The preamble to the constitution of India seeks to assure the unity and integrity of the Nation and the dignity of the individual. The foremost condition for the realisation of these objectives is the prevalence of peace, harmony and, above all, the rule of low. Even though 'public order' and 'police' are primarily States' responsibilities, the Constitution casts ensuring that the obligation of protecting every State against internal disturbances and ensuring that the government in every State is carried on in accordance with the provisions of the Constitution. The ministry of Home Affairs discharges these obligations and has, therefore, a vital role to pay in the governance of the country as a whole.

Under the Government of India (Allocation of Business) Rules, 1961, the Ministry of Home Affairs comprises:—

— Department of Internal Security, dealing with Police, Law and Order and Rehabilitation;

— Department of States, dealing with Centre-State Relations, Inter-State Relations, Union territories and Freedom Fighters' Pension;

— Department of Official Language, dealing with the implementation of the provision of the Constitution relating to Official Language and the provisions of the Official Languages Act, 1963;

- — Department of Home, dealing with the notification of assumption of office by the President and Vice-President, notification of appointment of the Prime Minister and other Ministers, etc; and
- — Department of Jammu & Kashmir Affairs, dealing with the constitutional provisions with respect to the State of Jammu & Kashmir and all other matters relating to the State excluding those with the Ministry of External Affairs is concerned.

The Department of Official Language has a separate Secretary and functions independently. The Annual Report of the Ministry of Home Affairs does not, therefore, cover the activities of that Department. The Department of Internal Security, Department of States and Department of Home do not function in water-tight compartment.

They all function under the Home Secretary and are inter-linked. The Department of Jammu & Kashmir Affairs and the Department of Justice are also headed by the Home Secretary. The Department of Justice is a part of the Ministry of Law, Justice & Company Affairs. The Home Secretary is assisted by three Special Secretaries who discharge functions assigned to them. A proposal for the creation of a separate Department of North East Affairs within the Ministry of Home Affairs is under the consideration of the Government.

Information regarding the Minister, Secretary, Special Secretaries, Additional Secretaries and Joint Secretaries who held positions in the Ministry of Home Affairs (excluding the Department of Official Language) during the year 1998-99.

Law and order

The law and order situation, by and large, remained under control except in chronic trouble-spots in Jammu and in some State of the North East. In J&K, the level of militancy in the Kashmir Valley revealed a declining trend. However, there was an upsurge in militancy in the Jammu region. Increased dependence on alien mercenaries to induction of more sophisticated weaponry were the main features of militancy in the State of Jammu & Kashmir. In the North East, militant activities of insurgent and extremists groups and ethnic tensions continued to cause concern. A ceasefire was effected with the main insurgent group (NSCN-IM) in the North East.

Review of the internal security situation

The Ministry of Home Affairs has been interacting with the State Government on a regular basis in order to take stock of the low and order situation and the internal security scenario. A series of meeting were held with the Southern States on March 12,1998 and the Western State on August 28,1998. Subsequently, the Union Home Minister also convened a meeting of the Chief Ministers and senior officials of Northern State on October 14,1998. A meeting of the North Eastern States and Sikkim was held on November 6, 1998 at Guwahati. These discussions helped to create awareness among the States of the various dimensions of internal security problems and foster greater coordination of efforts among the Central and State governments.

Left-wing extremism

The States most affected by the Left- wing extremist activities include Andhra Pradesh, Bihar, Madhya Pradesh, Maharashtra and Orissa. The major groups involved in Left-wing extremism, which are operating in the country, are: CPML - People's War Group (PWG) in Andhra Pradesh, Madhya Pradesh, Maharashtra, Orissa, Karnataka and Tamil Nadu; the Maoist Communist Centre (MCC) and CPML- Party Unity (PU) in Bihar and, to some extent, West Bengal and CPML- Vinod Mishra

(VM) With its violence profile, mainly in Bihar. However, the over all violence perpetrated by Left-wing extremist groups registered a decline in 1998 as compared to the previous year with the States of Andhra Pradesh and Bihar reporting lesser number of incidents. Madhya Pradesh witnessed a considerable rise in the Left-wing extremist violence, which may perhaps be due to the spillover effect, following increased police action in Andhra Pradesh.

The Government attaches high priority to containing this menace by employing a double pronged strategy of strict law enforcement and special development initiatives in the affected areas. The Central Government has impressed upon the State Governments to take effective, well coordinated and integrated action which should include, among other measures, intensification of development activities, rapid improvement in roads and communication, implementation of land reforms, etc.

The Union Home Minister convened a meeting of the Chief Ministers of Andhra Pradesh, Madhya Pradesh, Maharashtra and Orissa on June 15,1998 at Hyderabad to review the action being taken by these States to curb the activities of Left-wing extremists. The following decisions were taken in the meeting:-

(a) The existing laws such as the National Security Act would continue to be invoked by the concerned State Governments. Simultaneously, the State Governments could examine enactment of a separate law to deal with Left-wing extremism.

(b) A comprehensive plan of action encompassing developmental activities as well as stepped-up security measures would have to be prepared by the States. Andhra Pradesh Government had already prepared such a plan which had been referred to the Planning Commission. Other State Governments should also prepare similar plans would be taken up with the Planning Commission for allocation of funds.

(c) A Coordination Centre would be set up at Hyderabad for reviewing the progress of thee Action Plan and coordinating the efforts of the State Governments.

In pursuance of these decisions, the Coordination Centre was constituted by the Ministry of Home Affairs on June 26,1998. The first meeting of the Coordinating Centre was held at Hyderabad on July 19, 1998. It was decided that the States would make more effective use of the existing provisions of law to counter the activities of extremists. It was also decided that the States would prepare a joint proposal for introducing direct communication network at the Police station and district level and upgrading roads systematically in the affected areas for faster communication. Follow up action has been initiated on all these decisions.

A scheme for financial assistance by the Central Government is under consideration. Requests for modern weapons and other equipments are also being considered on priority basis.

Liberation Tigers of Tamil Eelam (LTTE)

The unlawful activities of LTTE on Indian soil and their contacts and liaison with other extremist groups have been a cause of concern for the Government. The Government of Tamil Nadu and the Central Government were of the opinion that the opinion that the existing circumstances justified declaration of LTTE as unlawful association. Accordingly, the Central Government declared LTTE an unlawful association. Accordingly, the Central Government declared LTTE an 'unlawful association' by a notification published in the Unlawful

Activities (prevention) Tribunal for adjudication. The Tribunal, by its order dated the 13th November, 1998, confirmed the said notification.

Situation in Punjab

The State of Punjab has witnessed a remarkable turn around in social, political, cultural and economic spheres ever since trans-border terrorism in the State was effectively combated by the valiant people of Punjab and the Security Forces. Normalcy in the State is also reflected in the observance of various socio-cultural and religious activities by the people with enthusiasm. With the passage of time, election to various representative bodies like Parliament, State Legislative Assembly, Gram Panchayats, Municipal Bodies and Sikh Gurdwara Prabandhak Committee have been held in the State in smooth and peaceful manner.

With restoration of normalcy, the State of Punjab has witnessed accelerated peace of economic development. The 600 MW Ranjit Sagar Dam has been dedicated to the nation and power generation will commence in June, 1999 which will considerably enhance the availablity of electricity in the State. The cargo handling facilities at the Rajasanshi Air Port at Amritsar have been expanded to facilitate increased international trade activities. The Foundation Stone has been laid for setting up an oil refinery at Bhatinda at an estimated cost 16000 crores. Beside, as a result of fresh initiatives, new trends in agricultural and industrial sectors of the state have emerged which are reflected in diversification into food processing industries and a spurt in private sector investment, including foreign direct investment.

There is, however, no perceptible change in the desperate endeavours of the Pak based pro-'Khalistani' militants and their mentor, the Inter Service Intelligence of Pakistan, in reviving militancy in the State. Pro-

'Khalistani' militancy is now largely sustained by the ISI which continues to provide sanctuary, impart training, coordinate strategic and tactical moves, provide sophisticated arms and high grade explosives and actively assist in infiltration from across the border. Pakistan based top pro-'Khalistani' militants owing allegiance to various terrorist groups are under tremendous pressure from the ISI to step up violence in Punjab and neighbouring States by resorting to targeted killing of senior political leaders and government officials.

The Government of India has taken up this matter very firmly with the Government of Pakistan during the Home and Interior Secretary level talks between the two countries held at New Delhi on November 12,1998 as a part of the composite dialogue process between two countries. Pakistan has been told in no uncertain terms that it must abandon its State police of sponsoring terrorism in various part of India, and dismantle the infrastructure that exist in Pakistan for indoctrinating, training, arming, financing and then infiltrating mercenaries and militants into India from across the border.

The recent trend of infiltration mercenaries and militants into India from across the border. The recent trend of infiltration of Pak nationals into Punjab along with pro-'Khalistani' militants to carry out terrorist violence in Northern India has also been brought to the notice of Government of Pakistan. Pakistan has also been asked to execute International warrants of arrest issued by Interpol against top ranking militants/underworld operators and other fugitives from law of Indian origin sheltered in Pakistan.

The security Force are maintaining strong vigil along the International Border in Punjab and are fully prepared to thwart the evil designs of the left over pro-'Khalistani' militants based in Pakistan and some Western countries. There has been no over pro-'Khalistani' militants based in Pakistan and some Western countries.

There has been no major incident of terrorist violence in Punjab during the current year. In counter-terrorist operations, however, 22 extremists were arrested and a large quantity of sophisticated firearms, including rockets, hand granades, detonators, timer device and high grade explosives have been recovered from them.

The tercentenary celebrations of the ordaining of the Khalsa Panth have started in right earnest with the laying of the foundation stone of Khalsa Heritage Memorial Complex by the Panj Pyares at Anandpur Sahib on November 21,1998. Preparations for the celebrations are underway by almost all Sikh religious, intellectual and social organisations in Punjab, besides the SGPC and the State Government.

At the national level, the Human Resource Development Ministry has constituted a committee headed by the Prime Minister for preparation for this holy event. Sikh religious institutions and leaders have stepped up mobilisation efforts for the celebrations by organising "Gurmat Samagams and Khalsa Chetna Marches" in Punjab and elsewhere.

Vigilance along international border with Pakistan

As part of the strategy worked out by Government of India for effective policing of the Western border with Pakistan and for curbing infiltration/ex-filtration of mercenaries/ militants/drug traffickers from across the border for combating effectively trans border terrorism emanating from the other side of the border, fencing/ flood lighting of the Indo -Pak Border in the State of Punjab and Rajasthan has been taken up from 1988 inwards. A total length of 451 Kms of flood lighting in the entire Punjab sector, except some gaps in riverine areas, was completed in 1993. In Rajasthan sector, a length of 865 Kms has been fenced/flood lit upto December 31, 1997. The work of fencing/flood lighting in the remaining 167.60 Kms in Rajasthan sector is under execution and is likely to be completed by December 31, 1999.

Fencing/flood lighting of the international border in Jammu Sector, taken up in June, 1995, had to be suspended due to unwarranted and persistent firing from Pakistan in order to avoid unnecessary civilian casualties. The sealing of Jammu International border by fencing/ lighting and an intruder alarm system along the border has been planned and the work will be taken up at an appropriate time. Erection of fencing/flood lighting on a raised embankment along the Rann area of Gujarat is also being taken up in phases.

Border area development programme

For balanced development of remote and inaccessible border areas, ensuring effective administration in these resilience, the Border Area Development Programme (BDAP), was lunched in the 7th Plan period. This initiative was undertaken with limited scope and funds, covering the Western sector only, and has been continued during the 8th and 9th Plan period with extended coverage of the Eastern States which have international borders with Bangladesh. BADP is 100% Centrally sponsored scheme.

The total outlay for the 9th Plan period for this purpose is being finalised by the Planning Commission. The beneficiary State under the scheme are Assam, Gujarat, Jammu & Kashmir, Manipur, Meghalaya, Mizoram, Nagaland, Punjab, Rajasthan, Tripura and West Bengal, For the years 1998-99, the following States have been allocated the under-mentioned amounts under the Programme:—

Name of the state	Amount (Rs. crores)
Assam	4.27
Gujarat	8.88
Jammu & Kashmir	21.38
Manipur	4.00
Meghalaya	4.11
Mizoram	6.82
Nagaland	4.00
Punjab	8.82
Rajasthan	26.52
Tripura	11.34
West Bengal	31.36

International cooperation in combating organised crime, terrorism and drug trafficking.

The Ministry of Home Affairs, in association with other Central Ministries, has been actively engaged in evolving regional and international consensus for combating organized crime, terrorism and drug trafficking. Agreements have been signed with several friendly countries for cooperation in combating terrorism, organized crime and illicit trafficking in narcotic drugs and psychotropic substances in recent years.

A Mutual Legal Assistance Treaty in criminal matters with the Republic of France and an Extradition and Mutual Legal Assistance Treaty in criminal matters with the Republic of France and an Extradition and Mutual Legal Assistance Treaty in criminal matters with the Russian Federation were signed this year. Besides, drafts of mutual Legal Assistance Treaty and Extradition Treaty with UAE and Extradition Treaty with Germany, France, Bulgaria and Tunisia have been finalised and these are likely to be signed soon. Negotiations are in for signing treaties and agreements on Extradition and Mutual Legal Assistance with several other friendly countries.

The second meeting of the India-Nepal Joint Working Group on Border Management was held at New Delhi in June, 1998 in which several measures were agreed upon for ensuring that the open border and visa free travel regime between the two countries are not misutilised by elements inmical to either country.

In September 1998, at the behest of the Ministry of Home Affairs, the first meeting of the Indo-German Joint Working Group on Terrorism was held in Germany and useful exchange of information and views in the Indo-Canadian Joint Working Group on Terrorism held at Ottawa, Canada during the second week of November, 1998.

As a part of composite dialogue process with Pakistan on all outstanding issues having bearing on India-Pakistan relationship, talks were held with Pakistan on the subjects of "Terrorism and Narcotics" at New Delhi on November 12,1998. The Indian Delegation was led by the Union Home Secretary, Shri B. P Singh and the Pakistani Delegation was led by the Interior Secretary of Pakistan, Shri Hafeezullah Ishaq.

The attention of the Pakistani side was drawn to the uncontrovertible and irrefutable fact that it had consistently used terrorism as an instrument of State policy against India. Material evidence regarding involvement of Pakistan in instigating, indoctrinating, recruiting, training, financing, arming, infiltrating and controlling terrorists, foreign mercenaries and assorted underworld criminal elements with a view to using them in every way possible way for destabilizing India was presented to the Pakistani side.

It was told in no uncertain term to give up its relentless but futile pursuit of destabilizing India through State sponsored terrorism. It was also told to close down terrorist training camps functioning in Pakistan and to hand over to the Indian authorities, terrorist/fugitives from low of Indian origin sheltered in Pakistan.

Sena clashes

In Bihar, the landlords have formed various senas to counter the Left-wing extremists' menace. Prominent amongst these senas are the Ranvir Sena in Bhojpur, Buxar and Rohtas districts, Kisan Sangh in Patna, Jehanabad and Bhojpur districts, Gram Suraksha Dal mainly operating in Siwan district and the Sunlight Sena in Palamu, Garhwa, Aurangabad and Chhapra districts. In 1997, the Left-wing extremist groups clashed with the senas on 46 occasions. Quite a few atrocities on dalits by these landlords/upper caste senas came to notice.

Jain commission report

The finial report of the Jain Commission of Inquiry was received by the Government on March 7,1998 and the Government tabled it in Parliament on July 31,1998 together with the memorandum of action taken. The finial report was discussed by the Rajya Sabha on August 3 & 4, 1998 and the Lok Sabha on August 6, 1998.

Ram Janma Bhoomi- Babri Masjid issue

In term of the Supreme Court's judgement dated October 24, 1994 in the case of Dr. Ismail Faruqui vs. Union of India, the title suits relating to the Ram Janma Bhoomi-Babri Masjid dispute had been revived and hearing are continuing on day-to-day basis in the Lucknow Bench of the Allahabad High Court. The cases are at the stage of recording of evidence and examination of plaintiff witnesses. Thirteen such witnesses have been examined. Till the title suit are adjudicated for implementation of the final decision therein, the Central Government, as a statutory receiver, is maintaining the status-quo in the disputed area and would not allow any individual or organisation to violate the sanctity of the judicial orders.

Liberhan Ayodhya commission of inquiry

Proceeding before the Liberhan Ayodhya Commission of Inquiry set up to enquire, inter-alia, into the sequence of events leading to the events in the RJB-BM complex at Ayodhya on December 6,1992, are in progress. After completion of cross-examination of 29 prosecution witness by persons who were issued notices under section 8B of the Commission of Inquiry Act, the Commission has examined fifteen defence witnesses and five Commission's witnesses as on December 21, 1998 and further examination of the defence witnesses is continuing. The tenure of the Commission has been extended from time to time and the present tenure is upto June 30,1999.

3

Jammu & Kashmir

Security scenario in Jammu & Kashmir

Militancy in Jammu & Kashmir has taken a human toll of more than 19,000 lives in the last one decade (The higher figures quoted by Pakistani propaganda are patently false). The militants, aided and abetted by Pak ISI, have caused enormous damage to the Kashmir people and the state's economy. An elected Government was installed in the State in October 1996. The number of terrorist incidents registered a substantial decline during the years 1997 and 1998, including a significant fall in the number of civilian killings. This was despite the fact that there were deliberate attempts by the terrorists, and their mentors across the border, to step up violence in a desperate effort to try and thwart the restoration of the political and democratic process in the State.

Government policy on militancy in Jammu & Kashmir

The four principals of the Government's policy vis-a-vis the militancy in J&K are (i) deepening the democratic process, (ii) isolation of the militants and foreign mercenaries from the people, (iii) pro-active role within Jammu & Kashmir to neutralise the hostile designs of militants and foreign mercenaries and foreign mercenaries and (iv) galvanizing the development programmes. These are to be jointly achieved by the Union and State Governments.

Major incidents

Some of the major incidents of terrorism perpetrated by the militants recently include:—

— Killing of 23 members of Kashmiri Pandits at Wandhama Village of Ganderable area (Srinagar) on the intervening night of January 25-26, 1998;

— Bomb explosion in Doda town on January 23,1998 injuring 12 persons of which 2 succumbed to their injuring;

— Killing of 26 persons at Parankote-Dhakikote village of Udampur District during the night intervening April 17-18,1998;

— Killing of 9 persons in Doda and 4 persons in Surankot of poonch district between May 4-6, 1998;

— Killing of 25 personsof a marriage party in Champnari Village (Doda) on June 19,1998;

— Killing of 16 persons in Shanua Thakrie/Sarwana villages (Doda district) on July 27,1998;

— Killing of 3 persons in Sildhar Dhok (Udampur distt.) on the intervening night of July 31 and August 1,1998; and

— Killing of 35 persons in Kalaban and Shatrundi areas of Chamba distt. (H.P) on August 3,1998.

— Killing of 20 persons in 3 separate incidents at Baljaran and Morha Pata in district Rajouri and Baryana in district Udampur on the intervening night of 19-20 February, 1999.

Militants and their sinister designs

These incidents demonstrate the manner in which the militants have tried to strike at soft targets through cowardly, sneak attacks in a bid to terrorise the people and vitiate the environment. Militancy presently is being run by foreign mercenaries through greater use of grenades, mines, IEDs and explosives in an apparent attempt to gain high visibility and to show the elected Government and the security forces in poor light.

The recent recovery of some remote controlled Air-bone Aerodynamics modules capable of carrying explosives in Rajouri also indicated the heinous designs of Pak ISI. Important leaders political activists/workers, surrendered militants, security forces personnel, VDCs, SPOs and Hindus are being targeted.

The strategy behind this is self-evident, viz., to try and curb the movement and activities of political representatives and cadres as well as voices advocating moderation and tolerance at the grass-roots level. It is also intended to intimidate and deter those who had been earlier involved in militant activities but would like to return to the mainstream.

More than 40 political workers/ activists and 109 surrendered/former militants and Special Police Officers have been killed in such targeted attacks during 1998. The killing of 23 Kashmiri Pandits, including women and children, on the January 25/26, 1998 in Wandhama village, the killing of 26 Hindus on April 17-18,1998 in Parankote- Dhakikot villages in Udampur district, 25 persons of a marriage party in Champnari on June 19,1998 appears to be aimed at thwarting attempts to bring back the migrants to the Valley and triggering off a fresh round of migration from the valley and Muslim majority areas of Jammu Division.

Situation in Rajouri/Poonch/Doda/Udhampur

The infiltration of men and material from the other side of the border is continuing inspite of increased vigilance of security forces. There are sign of planned efforts to try and extend the arc of violence to Rajouri, Poonch, Doda and Udhampur areas in the Jammu region, so as to create communal polarisation, develop pockets to be used as sanctuaries/hideouts in the sensitive regions along the LOC and project that there is insurgency and disaffection in all the Muslim areas of the State.

Additional security forces have region to check the growing activities of the militants in these areas. It was emphasised on all concerned that all efforts will have to be made to check infiltration and to ensure that the militants are not allowed to get entrenched in these areas.

Present trends

While, in terms of the continuing killing of civilians, there is obviously no room for complacency on the part of State and Central Government, there has been a definite of this are; the fact that a large number of people have been regularly flocking to the Secretariat and to the public representatives, a visible relaxation in the normal life in Srinagar and other parts of the Valley, Amarnath Yatra with huge participation of Yatris and also successful conduct of other yatras in the State, holding of major conferences in Srinagar, greater inflow of tourist traffic, reopening of hotels and cinema halls in the Valley, large attendance of people in meeting addressed by political leaders and large voter participation in the Lok Sabha elections of 1998, a definite increase in the flow of information about militants to the police and security forces, marked step-up in the involvement of the state police in anti-terrorist operation, etc. The number of incidents in higher and remote reaches of Rajouri, Poonch, Doda and Udhampur areas of Jammu region, however, show a disturbing increase.

Disturbed areas

Army and Para-military forces are deployed in Jammu & Kashmir for the aid of the Civil Administration and police in facing the militancy. The State Government has declared areas falling within 20 Kms. of the line of Control in the district of Rajouri and Poonch and the entire districts of Anantag, Baramulla, Badgam, Kupwara, Pulwama and Srinagar as disturbed areas, under the Armed Force (J&K) Special Powers Act 1990. This Act enables certain special powers to be conferred upon members of the Armed Forces in the disturbed areas to prevent terrorism/secessionist activities.

Unified headquarters

There are two Unified Headquarters working under the Chairmanship of the Chief Minister at Jammu and Srinagar with the Core Commanders of the XV and XVI Corps as Security Advisors to the Chief Minister, Jammu & Kashmir for coordinating and sharing security related intelligence, and working out current strategies for countering terrorism and militancy to the area, as also to coordinate operations and deployment of Security Forces. The State Government has been requested to further strengthen the coordinating mechanism of UHQ to have a still more effective role. At lower levels, the district administration coordinates with the Security Forces to counter terrorist activities.

Operation group

An Operations Group under the Chairmanship of the Special Secretary (J&K) has been set up in the Ministry of Home Affairs to have a periodical review of the security situation in Jammu & Kashmir, including the intelligence inputs, deployment of CPMFs and coordination of the internal security related operations with the officers of Government of Jammu & Kashmir, para-military forces, Ministry of Defence, army , the intelligence agencies, and the Department of Jammu & Kashmir Affairs of the Ministry of Home Affairs constituting this Group. A similar Group for periodic meetings on intelligence sharing related to Jammu & Kashmir has also been constituted under the Special Secretary.

High level meeting of May 18,1998

A meeting was organised by the Home Minister on May 18,1998 with Defence Minister, Governor, Jammu & Kashmir and senior officers of Government of India, State Government, Army and Central Para- Military Forces which discussed the situation and problems in detail. A Special Group was constituted under the Chairmanship of Special Secretary (J&K) (with DGMO Army, DG, BSF, DG, J&K Police, Special Director, IB and Joint Secretary, Department of Jammu & Kashmir Affairs of the Ministry of Home Affairs as members to go into issues of strategies and tactics for checking infiltration and flushing out militants as well as to consider necessary upgrading of security forces in terms of weapons-mobility, etc,. and to prepare a Special Action Plan to tackle militancy in Jammu & Kashmir.

The Special Group conducted a detailed study in the matter, held discussions with the various authorities, visited Jammu & Kashmir and prepared a detailed Action Plan to counter militancy in the State. A number of High Level meetings were also held from time to time to discuss issues related to operationalising the action plan and to review the internal security situation in Jammu & Kashmir and the adjoining areas of Himachal Pradesh.

Strategy for tackling militancy

As one of the major prongs of a multi-pronged strategy to tackle militancy in Jammu & Kashmir, the Government has adopted a multi-dimensional approach which includes, inter-alia, strengthening the border management to check infiltration, neutralising plans of militants by proactive action against them in the hinterland within Jammu & Kashmir, gearing up intelligence machinery, protecting the minorities, greater interaction with the border population and greater functional integration through an improved institutional framework at the Unified Headquarters and at lower levels, etc. An Action Plan has accordingly been prepared to tackle militancy in Jammu & Kashmir and, after the incidents in Chamba, it was decided to integrate the anti-militancy efforts in HP with the Action Plan strategy.

A total provision of Rs.560.47 crores has been made for the security forces including the State Police, spreading over to three years, to make the action plan functional, out of which Rs.188.50 cores has been earmarked for the current year. Besides, the Central Government is reimbursing Security Related Expenditure (SRE) to the State of Jammu & Kashmir.

Ever since the well crafted macro level action plan to contain militancy in Jammu & Kashmir which includes containing spill over militancy in Himachal Pradesh and the functioning of the Ops group headed by Special Secretary (J&K), has been made operational, there have been encouraging result evidenced by statistics. During the calender year 1998 the total number of militants killed was 999.

Similarly, the total number of foreign militants killed in Jammu & Kashmir during 1998 is 319 as compared to the previous year's 197 which was the highest in any previous calendar year. A comparison of the terrorism-related statistic with that of last calendar year. reveals that incident this year were 2932 against 3420 last year, which indicates a downward trend. Similarly, the number of civilians killed has been 867 as compared to 938. Of the 867 civilians killed 723 were Muslim and 144 were non-Muslims.

However, the number of security force personnel killed is 232 against 185, which is on the higher side and this is because of the increased number of anti-militancy operations. (However, in this regard it may be pointed out that the number of security forces killed was higher in 1994). The number of persons arrested under substantive law in 1998 was 457.

Strengthening and modernisation of Jammu & Kashmir Police

An amount of Rs.5.00 crore has been released to the State Government of Jammu & Kashmir for the modernisation and upgradation of Jammu & Kashmir Police in its efforts to equip itself with modern and sophisticated equipments. In additional to the above, the Action Plan for tackling militancy in Jammu & Kashmir, approved in principle, has an outlay of Rs,192.53 crores for strengthening and modernisation of Jammu & Kashmir Police out of which Rs.38 crore are to be spent in the current financial year. These funds are to be provided as special SRE (Security Related Expenditure) for the Action Plan.

SRE parameters review committee

An amount of Rs.154.96 crore was reimbursed to the State Government during the year 1997-98 on account of security related expenditure in respect of various items. As the items admissible for reviewing the guidelines for reimbursement of security related expenditure to the State of Jammu & Kashmir-both item-wise and norm-wise. The Committee has recommended enlargement of the coverage of the SRE Scheme. As per the recommendations of the Committee a Standing SRE Committee on Jammu & Kashmir has been constituted which would also look into spill over of militancy/ terrorism into Himachal Pradesh.

Banning of JKLF

The Jammu and Kashmir Liberation Front, a militant organisation, was declared as an unlawful association under section 3 of the Unlawful Activities (Prevention) Act, 1967 vide notification dated February 17,1998. The ban has since been confirmed by the Unlawful Activities (Prevention) Tribunal vide order dated August 14,1998.

Publicity and propaganda

Pakistan has contained its self-evidently false but assertive propaganda and vilification campaign against India by openly misutilising its official media and diplomatic channels with a clear intent of bringing Jammu & Kashmir into sharper international focus. Pakistan has stepped up its effort to eulogise the terrorists and their activities. Given Pakistan's unrelenting propaganda and its efforts to internationalise the Kashmir issue in the post Pokran II phase, it has become imperative on our part to amplify our efforts to expose Pakistani's continued involvement in, and sponosorship of, secessionist and terrorist violence in jammu & Kashmir. We also need to highlight the fallacy in Pakistan's arguments about the Accession, and the UN Resolutions, and project the functioning of popular democracy in Jammu & Kashmir within the federal framework of the Union of India.

While our media efforts are continuing, a draft of an Approach Paper on Media Strategy in respect of Jammu & Kashmir is under consideration of the Government, inter alia, to ensure that the people of India, especially in the State of Jammu & Kashmir, as well as the international community are able to get a better feel of ground realities prevailing in Jammu & Kashmir and informed about the true perspective of the Jammu & Kashmir issue. The electronic and print media are being used and expanded in an effective and meaningful manner so as to reach the people in far flung areas of Jammu & Kashmir.

Economic development in Jammu & Kashmir

The Central Government has assisted the State Government in meeting the difficult situation due to the ongoing militancy. The plan outlay of the State of Jammu & Kashmir is being protected by the Centre by bridging the Non-plan gap. The Annual Plan 1998-99 of Jammu & Kashmir was approved at Rs. 1900 crores, a step up 20% over the previous year. Central assistance for the Plan would be Rs.2459.24 crores.

Of this Rs.850 crores is by way of Special Central Assistance and Rs. 250 crores. Of this, Rs.850 crores is by of Special Central Assistance and Rs. 250 crores as Special Plan Assistance. However, as the additional resource mobilisation could not be achieved, the plan size has been fixed at Rs. 1750 crores.

Some of the important initiatives taken accelerating the pace of development and economic activities in the State are as under:—

— Construction of a 290 Km. Railway line from Udhampur to Baramulla is under progress, in both the Valley & Udhampur ends of the line.

— In order to fully meet the peak power requirement of the State throughout the year, the Central allocation of power to the State has been increased to 876 MW, and the allocation was protected during the winter season when the generation of power decreases. All the 4 units of Uri Hydel Project (4x120MW) have been commissioned during 1997 and the work on Dulhasti Hydel Project (130 MW) has been resumed in April, 1997.

— An amount of Rs.87 crores has been approved for reconstruction of damaged bridge in Jammu & Kashmir in the plan outlay in 1998-99.

— An amount of Rs. 25 crores has been approved by the Planing Commission in the Plan Outlay in 1998-99 for the development of the Dal Lake.

Debt relief

A scheme for grant of debt relief to borrowers (having borrowings less than Rs.50,000) of Jammu & Kashmir, in the transport, tourism, small scale industries and trade sector is under implementation. A sum of Rs. 50 crores was released to the State during the year 1997-98. For 1998-99, Rs.100 crores has been released to various banks and financial institutions to implement the Debt Relief Scheme.

For borrowers in Jammu & Kashmir whose original borrowing is over Rs.50,000 an Inter-Ministerial Committee, set up under the Chairmanship of the Special Secretary (J&K), has examined the issue and given its recommendation on relief required to be provided. These recommendation of the Committee are being processed in consultation with other Departments.

Employment

The issue of providing employment to unemployed educated youth of Jammu & Kashmir has been receiving increased attention of the Central/State Government. As a result of special measures taken by the Central Government, more than 12,000 persons from Jammu & Kashmir have been employed in various Central Government offices/PSUs as well CPOs. Of this, more than 10,000 have been recruited by various CPMFs.

The Department of Personnel & Training has issued instructions for extending the age limit relaxation upto 5 years for Jammu & Kashmir youth with a view to increasing their intake in Central jobs. This relaxation has now been extended till December 31,1999. Given the limited employment opportunities with the Government/

PSUs at Central and State level, special emphasis is being laid on employment oriented schemes like PMRY, J&K Self-employment Scheme (JKSES), etc.

Rehabilitation of widows and orphans

In 1995, the Government of Jammu & Kashmir had set up a Council, for rehabilitation of widows, orphans, handicapped and old-aged persons adversely affected by militancy as a registered body under the Societies Registration Act. The Council had a corpus of Rs. 6.28 crores as on April I, 1998, which included Rs.4.00 crores as contribution from Government of India and Rs. 1 crores from the Prime Minister's National Relief Fund. The State Government will be contributing a sum of Rs. 2.00 crores as its share towards the corpus during the year.

A significant number of beneficiaries have covered under the rehabilitation scheme. A total of 255 old aged persons, 672 widows and 15552 orphan students have been covered under various welfare schemes. An expenditure of around Rs. 21 lakhs has been incurred on this account till date.

Revival of tourism in the Kashmir valley

Due to the disturbed situation arising out of militancy in the State, tourism became one of the worst hit sectors and a large extent of tourism related infrastructure got damaged. However, with the installation of a popular Government in the State in October 1996, there has been a slow but steady improvement in the number of tourists to the State.

The Amarnath Yatra, 1998 has shown an unprecedented record of 1,49,920 pilgrims. Significantly, the tourism and travel industry has once again shown an enthusiasm for revival of their business. Attempts to sustain this enthusiasm are being mad by the State

Government of India. The Prime Minister's package for the State also includes a debt relief scheme for the affected persons in this sector. The Ministry of Tourism, Government of India, has set up a Special Committee on Revival of Tourism in the State of Jammu & Kashmir which has since submitted its first draft report.

Rehabilitation of migrants and militants

In the initial phases of the terrorist violence in Jammu and Kashmir, the externally aided and inspired militants created a situation as a consequence of which a vast majority of Kashmir Pandits and a sizeable number of Sikhs, other Hindus as well as some Muslims, migrated from the Valley in 1990. These migrant families are now staying mainly in Jammu Division, which some have migrated to other parts of the Country.

It is hoped that these migrants would return to the Valley as soon as condition reasonably conducive for their return are established and the policy towards the migrants is based on this premise. Hence, permanent rehabilitation of the migrants outside the State is not envisaged.

Consequently, the thrust of the police has been to ensure that difficulties and hardships facing the migrants are mitigated and the needy families are provided with a reasonable amount of sustenance and support. These migrants are being given relief by the State/UTs where they are temporarily residing.

A sizable number of migrants are staying in relief camps in Delhi and Jammu and necessary civic amenities such as facilities like water, electricity, sanitation, etc, have been provided to them. The living condition of the migrants in these camps are closely monitored by the Ministry of Home Affairs. On its part, the State Government has enacted the J&K Migrants Immovable

Property (Preservation, Protection and Restraint on Distress Sales) Act, 1997 on June 2, 1997 to prevent distress sale of immovable property by the migrants. The State Government has also enacted the J&K Migrants (Stay of Proceedings) Act, 1997 on June 2, 1997 to stop under harassment to migrants due to litigation in absentia. These two statutes would provide further relief to the migrants.

Both the Central Government and the State Government are keen on the return of the migrants to their homes and hearths, and the State Government has been asked to prepare a detailed action plan in this regard.

The Government of Jammu & Kashmir has informed the Centre that safe and honourable return of migrants to their native places in the Valley is a matter of top-most priority for the State Government and that the Government is drawing a detailed plan in this regard. The State Government has constituted subcommittee of Ministers of Revenue, Law, Finance and Tourism to examine the whole issue and make recommendations.

As an element of the overall strategy to resort normalcy in the State, a Surrender Policy was announced in August 1995 in order to offer encouragement and incentives to militants to leave the path of violence and join the mainstream. The Surrender Policy was revised by the State Government in June, 1997. The cash incentive for surrendered arms, ammunition and equipment was increased substantially by more than 100 percent for most of the categories.

The stipend for surrendered militants was also increased to Rs.1800/-per month from the day of surrender to the day of resettlement or for a period of 12 months, whichever is earlier, as compared to the earlier, as compared to the earlier policy which allowed a stipend of Rs.1500/- per month to the surrendered militants who were undergoing training at the Rehabilitation Centres.

Since the announcement of the Surrender Policy in 1995, 1515 militants have surrendered till September 30,1998. These militants have also surrendered a large quantity of arms and ammunition. From 1990 onwards a total of 2847 militants have surrendered. The Government of India had approved raising of two battalions for the Central Para Military Force mainly comprising these surrendered militants. 812 militants, who have surrendered, have been recruited in these battalions so far. These surrendered militants will also be covered under Prime Minister's Rozgar Yojna or State Self-Employment Scheme for providing them with a permanent source of livelihood.

4

North-East

North-East India comprises the State of Arunachal Pradesh, Assam, Manipur, Meghalaya, Mizoram, Nagaland and Tripura. The region accounts for 8% of the total land surface of India and has a population of 316 lakhs (1991 census).

North-East has been a focus of attention as far as the Ministry of Home Affairs is concerned. A separate division in the Ministry looks after the entire gamut of issue relating to the seven North-East (including Sikkim and North Bengal), boundary matters with neighbouring countries, border management (including border roads/ fencing), matter relating to the North-Eastern Council coordination of developmental issues relating to the North Eastern State and Sikkim, monitoring of the Prime Minister's package for the North East, North-East Council, tribunals under the IMDT Act, a special scheme for modernisation of police force in the North-East, reimbursement of security related expenditure for the North-East, implementation of the Assam and Bodo Accords and MOUs on Karbi Anglong and North Cachar Hills Autonomous Councils, publicity in the North East, etc. A proposal for creation of a separate Department of North-East Affairs in the Ministry of Home Affairs is also under consideration of the Government.

Government's approach to the North- east

The first Prime Minister of India, Shri Jawaharlal Nehru, had a vision of North East India in which the tribals would be allowed to develop according to their own genius. In his view the development of North-East was to be pursued within the broad framework of the following five fundamental principles:-

— People should develop along the lines of their own genius and we should avoid imposing anything on them. We should try to encourage in every way their own traditional arts and culture.

— Tribal right on land and forests should be respected.

— We should try to train and build up a team of their own people to do the work of administration and development. Some technical personnel from outside will, no doubt, be needed especially in the beginning. But we should avoid introducing too may outsiders into tribal territory.

— We should not over-administer these areas or overwhelm them in a multiplicity of schemes. We should rather work through and not in rivalry with their own social and cultural institutions.

— We should not judge results not by statistics or the amount of money spent, but by the quality of human character that is evolved.

The incorporation of the Sixth Schedual in the Constitution of India and the formation of District Councils to meet the political aspirations of the tribals was a recognition of the distinctive set-up in North- East region. However, this did not fully meet the aspirations of the tribals.

The grant of separate Statehood or Union territory status to the hill areas was a new approach that changed the pattern of administration. The other fundamental changes which were witnessed in 1971-72 were elimination of the role of Zonal Councils, setting up of North-Eastern Council by an Act of Parliament and the North-East areas as an administrative concept.

The next major change in approach was evolved during 1996 when the elements of a National Strategy for the North-East Region were laid out in the Statement of the Prime Minister on 27 October, 1996 after his visit to the seven North-Eastern States.

This statement was laid on the Table of both the House of Parliament. The elements included in this strategy were:—

To tackle insurgency

— Office of unconditional talks

— Violence to be put down with a firm hand

— Improved relations with neighbouring countries

(b) Accelerated infrastructure development and stress on employment schemes.

— Shukla Commission

— Bopparai Committee

— 10% of Budget earmarked for NE by all Central Ministries

— EAS extended to all blocks

— Full telecome and electronic media coverage

— Improved credit flow

— New Industrial Policy

— Development of Tourism

— Improvement in rail services

— Package for schemes announced (Rs.6100 Crores)

(c) Good government and decentralization

— Transperancy / accountability

— Strengthening Autonomous District Councils

— Implementation of Panchayat Raj

— Further decentralization

(d) Foreigners issue

— Repeal of ineffective laws

— Strengthening of legal and administrative measures

— Better border management

(e) Ethnicity

— Better understanding of identity issues of various tribles

— Removing perceptions of neglect and alienation.

Modernisation of police force in north-east

The Ministry of Home Affairs has been giving top priority to the modernisation of the State Police forces in the North-East. This includes special training, modern arms, better mobility, upgraded communications, improved intelligence and housing facility. During 1996-97 and 1997-98, the total releases for modernisation of police force amounted to Rs.47.57 crores of which Rs.35 crores was given in kind. In future, the Central assistance for modernisation of police forces in North-East would be giving, as far as possible, in kind.

Harnessing of administration

Insurgency cannot be contained by bullets alone. It has been recongnised that the civil administration in the North-East States has a very significant role in countering insurgency. The areas that deserve special focus of the civil administration include speedy grievance redressal, mass mobilisation of social and economic resources, greater transparency and accountability and speedy economic development. The army and para-military forces involved in counter-insurgency operations should concentrate on better border management, neutralisation of the operations launched by agencies hostile to India and providing area security to enable the local authorities to play their basic role.

Action plan for the north-east : a blue print

It has also been realised that "Look North-East Policy" should be the fundamental guiding principle for the Central Ministries. Infrastrutural development, particularly Inter-State communication and transport should be speeded up as a part of economic upgradation and a carefully designed industrialisation programme suited to the resources available in the region drawn up. It has also recognised that undue centralisation of authority for allocation of funds at the State level needs to be dismantled in a time-bound manner.

Decentralisation of economic development is extremely important because these small States in the North-East were created precisely to fulfill the aspirations of autonomy. Also, having regard to the fact that the North-Eastern States have almost 98% of the external boundaries touching the neighbouring countries of Bhutan, China, Myanmar and Bangladesh, it is equally important to develop close and friendly ties with the neighbouring countries and also set up institutional arrangements for cooperation on mutual security concerns.

Some of the other important decisions taken during the year in regard to the North-East are:—

Approval of the guidelines for reimbursement with effect from 1st April, 1995 of excess security related expenditure incurred by insurgency affected North

Eastern States. After preliminary scrutiny and subject to audit, the State mentioned below have been reimbursed the amount indicated below for the period 1995-96 to 1997-98:—

— Assam — Rs. 78.86 crores

— Nagaland — Rs. 35.61 crores

— Tripura — Rs. 28.55 crores

— Manipur — Rs. 19.43 crores

The proposal for restructuring of the North-Eastern Council was also approved by the Union Cabinet. The salient features of the restructuring are:—

— Sikkim shall be included in the Council.

— The Government, who are the Constitutional Heads, shall cease to be Members of the Council.

— Besides the Chief Ministers of the North-Eastern States, the Council shall consist of three Members to be nominated by the President of India.

— The Council shall function as a Regional Planning Body for the North-Eastern Area. Instead of being merely an advisory body, the Council shall have such powers as may be delegated to it by the Central Government.

— While formulating regional plans, the Council shall give priority to schemes and projects benefiting two or more States, except in the case of Sikkim which does not have common geographical boundary with other member State of the Council. The Council shall formulate and implement State specific projects and schemes for Sikkim.

— No scheme shall be placed before the Council unless it has been recommended by a screening committee consisting of the Secretary of the Council as Chairman and the Planning Secretaries of the States of the North-Eastern area as members. This provision is intended to ensure that the schemes selected by the Council for implementation have a regional character and reflect the felt needs of the member States of the Council.

The NCE (Amendment) Bill was introduces in the Rajya Sabha on December 8,1998.

The International Fund for Agriculture Development (IFAD) project at an estimated cost of Rs.159.40 crores has been introduced with the overall objective to improve the livelihood of vulnerable groups in a sustainable manner through improved management of their resource base in a way that contributes to protecting and restoring the environment. The project will pursue its objectives as per the following strategy:-

— capacity building of communities and participating agencies comprising village institutions, savings and credit self-help groups and development of skills in participatory processes for NGOs and staff of Government and private sector service providers;

— economic livelihood activities comprising irrigation, crop development, horticulture/perennial crop development, forestry, livestock, fisheries, extension and technology transfer, adaptive research, non-farm enterprises and strategy development and new products development;

— community based bio-diversity conservation comprising protection of sacred groves and buffer zone management around protected areas;

— social sector activities comprising drinking water, community health care and schools agriculture programme;

— village rods and rural electrification comprising upgrading and construction of village link roads and provision of electricity to villages; and

— project organisation and management including monitoring and evaluation.

Talks with the All Assam Students Union (AASU) and the Government of Assam on the review and implementation of the Assam Accord continued in a cordial atmosphere. A field visit to the border areas of Assam and Bangladesh was also organised. A Sub-Committee of main Committee was constituted to look in to the proposals concerning Clause VI of the Assam Accord. The Sub-Committee is expected is expected to give its report by April, 1999.

Tripartite talks with the Bodo Groups and the Government of Assam were also held. For the first time, non-Bodo Groups, who constitute the majority of the population in the Bodoland Autonomous Area, were invited for expressing their views on resolving the Bodo problem. The discussions are continuing.

Notification were issued under the Unlawful Activities (Prevention) Act, 1997 declaring ULFA and NSCN as unlawful associations on November 23,1998 and NDFB on November 26,1998, respectively.

The ceasefire with the NSCN (I/M) was extended for a period of one year w.e.f August 1, 1998. It was also clarified to the NSCN (I/M) that the ceasefire was between the Government of India and the NSCN as an organisation. Shri Swaraj Kaushal was appointed as a political representative on behalf of the Government of India for talks with the NSCN (I/M). A unilateral ceasefire against NSCN (Khaplang Group) was also announced by the army with effect from November 15,1998 for a period of two month to enable them to discuss and formally accept the offer of ceasefire. This was further extended by three months and has been reciprocated by the NSCN (K).

Helicopter Service have been introduced in Meghalaya with 75% funding by the Ministry of Home Affairs w.e.f. February 15,1999.

The continuing inter-factional clashes, kidnappings and large scale extortions by NSCN (I/M) slightly vitiated the atmosphere of the ceasefire. It is hoped that the NSCN (I/M) will demonstrate its sincerity towards the ceasefire by stopping such clashes and kidnappings and also extortions which cause considerable hardship to the people of Nagaland. The Naga Hoho have themselves expressed concern at the large scale extortions by the NSCN (I/M) and have called upon the NSCN (I/M) to desist from such illegal collections.

Ethnic conflict in Churachandpur District, Manipur

The ceasefire negotiated at the initiative if the State Government has happily been converted into a permanent peace accord. The Kuki and Paite tribals in Churachandpur district are now at peace. The Government of India sanctioned Rs.4.67 crores for the rehabilitation of the 4672 families affected by the ethnic clashes.

Insurgency in Manipur

Important outfits operating in Manipur are Revolutionary Peoples Front (RPF) Peoples Liberation Army (PLA), United National Liberation Front (UNLF), peoples Revolutionary Party of Kangleipak (PREPAK), Kangleipak Communist Party (KCP), Kanglei Yawl Kanba Lup (KYKL), Kuki National Organisation Socialist Council of Nagaland (Isak/Muivah). The valley districts are affected by Meitei UGs and hill districts are affected by Naga and Kuki UGs.ZRA is largely operating in Churachandpur District.

Meitei UGs are maintaining a high level of violence. One of the disturbing features of their violence profile is attacks on the security forces, particularly those inducted from outside. However, the total number of incidents up to November 26,1998 has come down to 155 as against 220 last year. The number due to insurgent violence is also only 103 as compared to 129 last year.

A part from this, the State is infested with the Naga insurgency as NSCN (I/M) has its area of influence in hill district of Manipur. The Kuki militants are also operating in these districts and their activities, which include attack on security forces, are a cause for concern.

The State has to cope with the problems of Naga-Kuki ethnic conflict, also. The decision of the State Government to consider creation of a separate Sadar Hills Revenue district led to protest by Naga organisations including imposition of month a long economic blockade on National Highway-39. Although this blockade was lifted on June 24, 1998, the upgradation of the posts of Additional D.C. and S.P., Kangpokpi empowering them to exercise powers of D.C. and S.P. in the area of the proposed Sadar Hills district in November, 1998 again created tension in the area.

The Naga-Kuki tension in the State is continuing. The areas of mixed population in Senapati, Ukhrul and Tamenglong Districts are particularly vulnerable from this point of view. However, the over-all number of violence has shown a declining trend. The total number of incidents is only 18 as compared to 49 in 1997. The total number of those killed has also come down to 33 as against 83 last year. The number of houses burnt has shown a declining trend at 36 this year as compared to 196 last year.

Migration of reangs from mizoram to Tripura

The Reang problem continues without any solution. AT present, 35995 Reangs are housed in refugee camps in Tripura. Central assistance amounting to Rs.748 lakhs towards reimbursement of expenditure incurred on maintenance of Reang refugees from Mizoram was sanctioned/released to the Government of Tripura. The Government of Mizoram was advised to take steps for creating an atmosphere conducive for the return of Reangs from Tripura. The Government of Mizoram was advised to take steps for creating an atmosphere conductive for the return of Reangs from Tripura. It is hoped that the new Government which has assumed office in Mizoram would give priority in resolving this issue.

Insurgency situation in Tripura

Tripura is facing low key insurgency for the last 19 years. Though around 20 armed tribal groups have been identified on ground donning such labels like All Tripura Tiger Force (ATTF), National Liberation Front of Tripura (NLTF), Tripura Tribal Volunteer Force (TTVF), Tripura Tribal Democratic Force (TTDF), Tripura Tribal Youth Force (TTYF), Tripura Liberation Organisation (TLO), All Tripura Bharat Suraksha Force (ATBSF), Tripura Tribal Action Committee Force (TTACF), Socialistic Democratic Front of Tripura (SDFT), All Tripura National Force (ATNF), Tripura Mukti Police (TMP), ETC., only 2 of them (ATTF and NLFT) are responsible for majority of killing and have some ideological mooring with main activities remaining confined to murders, looting, extortions, abductions, etc., for monetary gains. Broadly the entire Tripura Tribal Autonomous District Council (TTADC) area, having dense jungles and predominated by tribals, is affected by violence perpetrated by tribals extremists/miscreants. The violence is mostly targeted against non-tribals. Areas falling outside TTADC, predominated by non-tribals (Bengalis) are much less affected. The level of violence of tribal militants especially the NLFT has shown a significant increase in as much as there were 505 incidents upto the end of November, 1998 as compared to 303 incidents in 1997. The civilian casualities are 235 uptc November, 1998 as compared to 270 in 1997.

The number of security forces killed has come down to 25 in 1998 as compared to 50 in 1997. The number of insurgents killed was 14 this year, which was the same as last year. It has been noted that the tribal extremists have been attacking innocent civilians rather than security forces with a view to creating ethnic disturbance. The situation is kept under constant review.

Insurgency in Assam

United Liberation Front of Asom (ULFA), National Democratic Front of Boroland (NDFB) and Bodo Liberation Tiger (BLT) remained active for most of the year. Ethnic violence between Bodos and Santhals in lower Assam also caused misery in Kokrajhar and Bongaigaon districts of the State. The insurgent outfit were responsible for 635 incidents upto November, 1998 resulting in 499 deaths. However, coordinated action by Security Forces resulted in grater success against terrorists. 334 ULFA and 51 NDFB/ BLTF caders surrendered as a result of these efforts and those found eligible were inducted in Para-Military Forces.

Although the level of violence in Assam is higher than in previous years, this is primarily due to coordinated counter insurgency measures taken by Government to curb militancy and the retaliatory measures taken by terrorists. In view of the dwindling public support, the insurgence groups are increasingly targeting innocent civilians, including women and children with a view to terrorising the general public.

Relief measures were launched for persons displaced in Bodo-Santhal ethnic violence. 2.25 lakh persons were accommodated in the relief camps. A Central Health team visited Kokrajhar and Bongaigaon to access health requirement of the refugees. A total amount of Rs.6.74 crores was released for rehabilitation of victims of ethnic violence A team from the Ministry of Home Affairs led by Special Secretary (NE) also visited the relief camps in September, 1998.

Sikkim

The Dentists Act, 1948, the Pharmacy Act, 1948, the Indian Nursing Council Act, 1947, the Indian Medical Council Act, 1956 the Indian Poison Act, 1919 and the Government Savings Certificate Act, 1959 have been extended to the State of Sikkim. Sikkim is one of the Special category State in respected of Central funding. In order to boost communication, a Helicopter service between Bagdogra and Gangtok with 75% funding by Ministry of Home Affairs has commenced with effect from November 16,1998. Low and order situation in the State is normal.

Non-lapsable central resource pool

As announced by the Finance Minister in his Budget speech a Non-Lapsable Central Resource Pool has been created with a token provision of Rs.1 crore. The Planning Commission has identified approximately Rs.186 crores from various Ministries that are unable to spend 10% of their Budget for 1998-99 in the North-Eastern States. The Committee set up by the Planning Commission has already identified projects/schemes costing Rs.118 crores for funding with these resources. Formal sanction for release of the 93.10 crores to the North-Eastern States has been issued by the Ministry of Finance on February 15,1999.

Cooperation with neighbouring countries

The Union Home Secretary led an Inter-Ministerial delegation to Myanmar on 26-29 April, 1998 to further strengthen cooperation of two countries on matters of mutual internal security concerns. The previous Home Secretary level interaction with Myanmar had taken place in November, 1996.

The Union Home Secretary led another inter-Ministerial delegation to Bangladesh in November, 1998 Prior to this, the Home Secretary level interaction with Bangladesh had taken place in February, 1997 when the Home Secretary from Bangladesh had visited New Delhi. A Joint Working Group meeting with Bangladesh was held in New Delhi in AUGUST, 1998. These meeting helped further strengthen bounds of cooperation between two countries. The arrest of Anup Chetia, General Secretary, ULFA by Bangladesh Government is one example of such cooperation.

Fifth national games in Manipur

The Fifth National Games were organised in Manipur from February 14 to 25, 1999. The President of India inaugurated the games on February 14,1999. This is the first time a national event of this magnitude has been organised in any North Eastern State. Adequate security measures were made for the Games and the Ministry of Home Affairs provided additional units of Central Para Military Forces, anti-sabotage teams, sniffer dogs and other specialised equipment to ensure fool-proof security during the National Games.

5

Union Territories

The Constitution (7th Amendment) Act, 1956 replaced the States in Part C and Territories in Part D of the First Schedule by the 'Union territories' which, under Part II of the First Schedule (as amended) were then six in number. After subsequent amendment acts, there are seven Union territories, viz:—

— Andaman & Nicobar Islands

— Chandigarh

— Dadar & Nagar Haveli

— Daman & Diu

— Lakshadweep

— National Capital Territory of Delhi

— Pondicherry

The Union territories are administered in accordance with the provisions of articles 239 to 241 of the Constitution of India. Of the seven Union territories, the National Capital Territory of Delhi and Pondicherry have legislatures and Council of Ministers. The rest of the Union territories are without legislature.

The Union territories have a total outlay of 19701.28 crores for the Ninth Five Year Plan (1997-2002).

Andaman & Nicobar Islands

The Union territory of Andaman & Nicobar Islands, comprising 752 islands/islets and rocks, is situated between 6 and 14 north latitude and 92 and 94 east longitude in the Bay of Bengal. It has a total area of 8249 Sq.Kms. of which approximately 87% or 7171 Sq.Kms. is under forests. 36 of the islands are inhabited with a total population of 2,80,661 (as per the 1991 census). The tribal population, excluding Jarawas and Sentinelese, who could not be enumerated, is 26770.

Agriculture

The year under review witnessed improved agricultural production with food crops registering high growth rate. The total food productions was 1,03,928 tonnes upto November 1998 as against 1,04,654 5 tonnes in 1997-98. Under Soil Conservation Scheme, 94 hectares of land has been covered by November 1998. 2527 hectares for the year 1998-99.

Animal husbandary and fisheries

During 1998-99, under the Livestock Development Programme, 6, 67, 353 cases were treated upto October 1998. In addition, 488 veterinary health camps and 2644 mobile tours have been organised. 55 backyard poultry units were distributed to the tribals on 50% subsidy basis under Special Central Assistance Programme. 20 units of piglets were distributed to tribals on 50% subsidy basis.

As many as 10 schemes are currently under implementation for development of fisheries in the Union territory. Apart from imparting training to fishermen, financial assistance was extended to 30 fish farmers for renovation of their fish farms. Against the target of 27,700 tonnes during the year 1998-99, the production recorded up to November 1998 was 16,440 tonnes.

Roads and bridges

An outlay of Rs. 2736 lakh was made in 1998-99 for construction of 10 Kms. of rural roads, 9 Kms. of Andaman Trunk Road, 1Km. of new link in Port Blair headquarter, 15 Kms, of fair weather road and 5 permanent bridges. An expenditure of Rs. 1320.59 lakhs has been incurred upto November, 1998 and the works are in progress.

Public distribution system

Public Distribution System in Andaman & Nicobar Islands operates through a net work of 407 Fair Price Shops spread all over the territory.

Education

Educational needs of the population ate met through a network of 368 schools. Education facilities are available within 1 Km. of radius of all habitations. At present there are 43 Senior Secondary Schools and 2 Navodaya Vidyalayas, 37 Secondary Schools, 54 Middle Schools, 210 Primary Schools and 23 pre-primary schools and 1 Ashram School operating in the Union territory. Under the Special Adult Literacy Drive, 1760 persons were made literate during the year under report.

Forest

During the year under report, an area of 217 hectares was covered under enrichment plantation and an area of 230 hectares was covered under Cane and Bamboo plantation. 22 Kms. of roadside plantation was carried out under social forestry. Out of the plan outlay of Rs.972 lakhs for the financial year 1998-99, an expenditure of Rs.405.39 lakh has been incurred upto November 1998.

Health and family welfare

Out of the allocation of Rs.1895 lakhs for Medical and Public Health during the financial year 1998-99, an expenditure of Rs.1093 lakhs has been incurred upto November 1998. Health facilities continued to be provided in the territory through 125 health institutions.

Tourism

Various measures were taken to boost eco-friendly tourism in the territory. Thee Water Sports Tourism Complex has been augmented with various types of boats suitable for adventure water sports. Guest Houses at Mayabunder and Diglipur have also been inaugurated this year.

Power

Presently, 36 power houses scattered in various islands have a total generation capacity of 32.81 MW. Out of 547 villages, 501 villages have been electrified. Two bio-gas plants have been installed during the current year. The setting up of 20 MW Power Station at Bambooflat in South Andaman and the 2.25 MW capacity Hydro Electric Project at Kalpong river are in progress.

Shipping

The marine dockyard continued to undertake maintenance and repair of machineries of the vessels, survey of vessels and construction of small boats. Upto November 1998, 16 vessels were drydocked and 22 vessels were slipped in the slipways for repairs, Besides, 1371 jobs were undertaken. For inter-island transportation, 59 medium and small size vessels were operated. For operations between mainland and islands, 3 large vessels were made available.

Tribal welfare

During the current year, the major achievement included raising of cane and bamboo plantations in an area of 67.7 hectares, distribution of free text books to tribal students, distribution of blackguard poultry and reared birds to tribal families, construction of cargo shed and passenger hall at Malaca etc. Special attention was accorded to welfare and development of primitive tribal groups by providing free rations, food articles, clothing and medical aid.

Chandigarh

The Union territory of Chandigarh bears a urban cosmopolitan character. The territory is spered over an area of 114 sq.kms. with a population of 6.42 lakhs of which 86% reside in urban areas and 14% in the 22 villages of Chandigarh.

Culture and eduction

The UT Administration paid homage to the Nation on the 50th anniversary of our independence through creation of a City Museum. Chandigarh has four Government Arts and Science College, a Home Science College, a College of Education, a Teachers Training Institute, a Regional Institute of English and an Institute of Education. All villages and labour colonies have at last one primary school within one km. distance. Besides, 105 non-formal education centres provide education to those who cannot attend formal schooling. To encourage enrolment of SC children in rural areas, free uniforms, stationery, text-books, etc., are given to them.

Health

The entire population of Chandigarh is adequately covered by Health Service there are 4 big hospitals providing speciality and super speciality heath service viz., P.G.I., General Hospital, Government Medical College Hospital and Police Hospital. In addition, the Union territory has•22 Allopathic Dispensaries, 7 Rural Allopathic Dispensaries, one Chest Clinic and a Poly Clinic, in addition to one Primary Health Centre and 10 dispensaries. Eight mini Family Welfare Centres are also run various Social Organisations.

Welfare

The Social Welfare Department organises the National Social Assistance Programme and Integrated Child Development Services. The Department provides pensions to the aged, disabled and destitutes and widows. Other schemes include creches for the children of working mothers, scholarship to physically handicapped students, petrol/diesel subsidy and encouragement to inter-caste marriages. There are special schemes for SC students, girl students and women.

Dadra and Nagar Haveli

The Union territory of Dadra & Nagar Haveli is predominantly inhabited by member of Scheduled Tribes. It has a population of 1,38,477 of which about 80% belong to Scheduled Tribes. Thee Union territory is spread over an area of 491 sq.kms.and consists of 72 villages. Through the Union territory is being directly administered by the Central Government through an Administrator, the people's participation at grass-root level has been ensured with the establishment of 11 Gram Panchayats and a District Panchyat.

Education

During the year report, continued emphasis on universalisation of elementary education was given by the Administration. This included provision of free boarding and lodging, mid-day meals and free supply of uniforms and text-books to students from weaker sections. The intake capacity of the Training Institute was raised from 99 to 130 during the year under report. Besides, 94 teachers including 48 Trained Graduate Teachers (TGT) were appointed in various educational institutions.

Industry

During the year under report, 184 industrial units were registered in the Union territory. These are expected to provide employment to 4860 persons.

Transport

Sustained industrialisation has led to an increased demand for better and improved transportation. A Master Plan for constructing anew network of rods and widening of existing roads has been prepared to cater to this demand. Construction of a High Level Bridge has been taken up Surangi, Belugaon. Thee existing bridge over Pipariya river connecting the territory with Gujarat is being replaced by a new bridge which is nearing completion.

Welfare

The National Programmes of Poverty Alleviation continued to be given high priority. During the current year, 90 families were given assistance under Integrated Rural Development Programme (IRDP) and 14000 man-days were generated under Jawahar Rozgar Yojna (JRY).

Power

The demand for power is expected to increase from the existing 80 MW to 150 MW by the end of the Ninth Five Year Plan. The Central Electricity Authority has prepared a Master Plan for suitably augmenting the existing power generation capacity. This includes establishment of 66/11 KV and 220/66 KV sub-stations at Kharagpada and 66/11 KV sub-station at Rakholi. The work at these projects, which commenced last year, is in progress.

Tourism

In view of the growing tourist interest in the territory, development of Water Sports at Dudhani and Khandiv Van at Luhari is being completed. Other facilities like tourist cottages and tentage accommodation are provided for the tourists at selected places. Construction of the building for Yatri Niwas at Silvass has also been taken up.

Daman & Diu

The Union territory of Daman & Diu consists of two separate land blocks separated from each other by a distance of about 800 Kms. Daman & Diu have separate Municipal Councils and a common and a common District Panchayat.

Industry

During the year 1998-99,227 new industrial units were set up providing additional employment to about 10,000 persons. Another 17 industrial units (15 SSI & 2 MSI) are likely to be set up in the last quarter with additional employment to another 2,000 persons.

Tourism

Three lakes with island, garden, giant geneva fountains, boating facility and cafetaria have been developed in Daman District. In Diu District, Gandhipara fountain has been properly developed. Parts of these tourist facilities have been leased out to private entrepreneurs for providing such facilities as Health Club, Gymkhana, Swimming Pool, etc.

Technical training

Technical Training Institutes in both the Districts of the Union territory continued to provide vocational training to the students of VIII to X Standards in engineering, drawing, workshop technology and elements of mechanical engineering. 176 students of these Institutes passed out during the current year of which 138 got employed. A fresh batch of 238 students was admitted in the current year.

Health

During the current year, over 2536 children were immunized till October 1998. The Community Health Centre building constructed during the year was provided with modern equipment, such as Auto

Analyser, Sonography, etc. A number of health awareness programmes were also organised during the year under report.

Welfare

The tribal population is provided suitable assistance for their all round socio-economic development. Tribal students are also provided vocational and technical training through Technical Training Institutes. The Poverty Alleviation Programme was given the required thrust by creating increased opportunities for wage employment and providing financial assistance to the families living below the poverty line. This included grant of assistance to 34 families living below the poverty line and generation of employment under Jawahar Rozgar Yojna.

Lakshadweep

Lakshadweep is the smallest administrative unit in the country consisting of 36 islands scattered in the Arabian Sea. Only 10 out of these island are inhabited and the population according to 1991 Census is 51,707. About 93% of the population is Scheduled Tribes. The rate of literacy is 66.81%. The total land mass is 32 sq.kms. and it has an exclusive one district and are divided into 4 Tehsils.

Panchayat Raj

Village (Dweep) Panchayats and District Panchayats have been set up under the Lakshadweep Panchayat Regulations, 1994. A District Planning Committee also has been constituted. DRDA and Primary Education including other programmes have been transferred to District Panchayat.

Education

A number of schools, college and technical institutions provide free elementary and higher education to the people. Free boarding and lodging is also provided.

Health and family welfare

Health and medical facilities are provided by the Administration. Smallpox, malaria and filaria have been virtually eradicated. 100% coverage has been achieved under the Universal Immunisation Programme.

Industry

Coconut is the major produce of the territory and coconut husk is the main raw material available for the development of industries. There are about 14 factories based on coconut husk. A handicraft training centre is functioning in the Islands. A separate Khadi and Village Industries Board has been set up. About 435 Small Scale Industrial Units are functioning in the private sector with financial assistance from the Industries Department.

Transport

Lakshadweep is connected with mainland by sea and air. Two all weather ship and one fair weather ship, two catamarans, one oil tanker and four cargo barges provide the bulk of the shipping services in the Union territory.

Rural development

Under Integrated Rural Development Programme (IRDP) targetting the 45% population living below poverty line, 4085 families were given assistance till 31st October 1998. Development of Women and Childern in Rural Areas (DWCRA), Training for Rural Youth for Self Employment to become artisans are the main self employment programmes implemented through DRDA.

Fisheries

The territory is rich in marine sources. Modern mechanised fishing has replaced the traditional fishing. The islanders have taken to pole and line fishing using mechanised Pablo boats for tuna fishing. The Administration has introduced a scheme for providing mechanised boats on subsidy. HSD Oil is also given to fishermen at a highly subsidised rate.

Tourism

Tourism is a growing activity in the Islands and various promotional packages are organised by the Society for Promotion of Recreational Tourism and Sports. The bird sanctuary at Pitti Island has been formally declared as a protected bird sanctuary under the Wild Life Act. The Water Sports Institute at Kadmat Island organises Scuba diving course and marine health awareness programmes.

National capital territory of Delhi

Delhi, the National Capital Territory of the Union, has distinctive features and problems that evoke both pride and despair in equal measure. Delhi is spread over an area of 1483 Sq.Kms. However, less than 50% of the area, that is urban, sustains around 90% if its in population of 94,20 ,644 (as per 1991 census). There has, however, been a steep rise in population since then, mainly triggered by migration from various parts of the country. Delhi has, over the years, also seen urbanisation at a very rapid pace. These two phenomena have put unprecedented pressure in its infrastructure, civic amenities and low & order situation. Despite these pressures, Delhi's per capita net State Domestic Product is one of the highest in the country.

Under the Constitution (69th Amendment) Act, 1991, Delhi has been provided with a Legislative Assembly and a Consolidated Fund of its own. The Council of Ministers, headed by the Chief Minister aid and advise the Lt. Governor in the exercise of his functions. The Legislative Assembly has power to make laws for the National Capital Territory of Delhi with respect to any such matter as applicable to the States, except on matters relating to Public Order, Police and Land. These three subjects have been retained by the Central Government and are administered directly through the Lt.Governor.

Tackling problems of population, pollution, congestion, shortage of power, water housing, sanitation and above all, maintaining law and order have remained high priority areas for the National Capital Territory of Delhi.

Education

The Union territory Administration lays considerable emphasis on mass-literacy, non-formal education and improvement of quality of education at elementary and secondary levels. High priority has been accorded to the education of women, rural people and socially and economically backward students of the Scheduled Castes and Scheduled Tribes. Pre-primary education is mainly the responsibility of local bodies. There are in all 2002 Government Middle, Secondary Schools. Seven Middle Schools were opened and 15 schools upgraded from Middle to Secondary level.

Various schemes such as book-bank, free transport facilities to girl students in rural areas, free supply of uniforms, patrachar vidyalaya, vocational education and scholarships are continuing. In the field of higher education, 28 college are sponsored by Government of NCT of Delhi. These colleges are jointly financed by the Government of NCT of Delhi and the University Grants Commission. Perceptible improvement has been brought in the field of technical education and training. Private sector has been associated to enhance the production of trained technical manpower. Capacity expansion and quality improvement of technical programmes at Degree, Diploma and Certificate levels as also Craftsmen Training have been achieved through community polytechnic schemes and involvement of private sector. These programmes were implemented with the effective utilisation of World Bank assistance for Technical Education and Vocational Training.

Health and family welfare

With a view to providing universal medical facilities to all residents of Delhi, the Government of Delhi is running 11 hospitals besides number of campaign health Centres, dispensaries and poly clinics. During the year 1998-99, a number of campaigns and programmes like Matri-Surakasha Abhiyan, Shravan Shakti Abhiyan, Thalassemia screening among childern, Pulse Polio Programmes, Delhi Arogya Nidhi and Motiabind Mukti Abhiyan, Prohibition of smoking at public -phases, Centralised Accident Trauma Service and Sunday Clinic for senior citizens, etc., were launched so as to provide adequate and proper health care for the residents of the Union territory. A food & drug laboratory has set up to facilitate analysis of drug and food articles on order to check adulteration.

Industry

The NCT of Delhi has been divided into five zones with a view to ensuring effective development of industries. Consequent upon the Hon'ble Supreme Court's order for closure of 168 polluting industrial units, steps have taken to relocate them outside the city limits. The Government has approved the issue of provisional eligibility letter to 10,265 applicants who had applied for 935 acres of land in village Bawana and Halombi Kalan. Additional land has also been identified for acquisition.

The foundation stone for the construction of 'Udyog Sadan' at 4 acres of land at Patparganj, Delhi has been laid. The construction of 400 flatted factories has commenced at Jhilmil at Tahirpur Industrial Estate. A Centre for Information and Technology in Computer Applications and Tool Design has been set up at Tool Training Centre at Wazirpur in order to provide latest technical information on contemporary technology in the field of tool design and computer application to the industry.

The Hi-tech Vocational Training Centre is providing the latest technology in the field of electronics, automobile and engineering industries. The Delhi State Industrial Development Corporation has developed industrial estates at Mangolpuri, Kirti Nagar and Okhla for setting up engineering, packaging and electronic incident industries. The Corporation has also completed the construction of 3 facility centres at Narela Industrial Complex.

Transport

In a major city like Delhi, maintaining an efficient Transport System has always been, and is, a challenge of sorts. Around 524 buses including Blue Line buses and D.T.C/Km. Scheme buses have been nationalised and about 5751 buses are now being run by Delhi Transport Corporation including 2645 of them under Km. Scheme. An action plan for Vehicular Population Control has been prepared identifying short, medium and long-term measures for the control of vehicular pollution in Delhi.

Welfare

Several schemes for the welfare of children, women, physically handicapped persons and other weaker and under privileged section of society are being operated by the Government. 14 statutory homes/institutions for the children (which include 3 observation homes and 11 juvenile homes), 10 non-statutory institutions and 28 ICDS projects for welfare of women and children are being run. There are institutions which also provide training and education to mentally retarded children.

The Delhi Scheduled Castes Finance and Development Corporation provides finances and promotes the economic activities of scheduled castes/ scheduled tribes living below the poverty line.

Delhi Vidyut Board

The Delhi Vidyut Board has taken steps to rationalise electricity supply in Delhi. Unauthorised colonies, which had come up prior to 1993, have been allowed legal connections with a view to reducing that and pilferage. Single point supply has been installed in industrial complexes. Similarly, in order to augment generation, 300 MV Plant at I.P.Estate has been approved for commissioning by BHEL on turn key basis. Steps are being taken to allow private sector participate in distribution of energy in Delhi.

Sales tax

Sales Tax collection target of Rs.2450 crores has been fixed for the financial year 198-99. Till 31st October 1998, a sum, of Rs.982.03 crores has been collected which shows an increase of 7.97% over the same period.

Tourism

Efforts to promote Tourism and fully tap the tourism potential of the historic and rich cultural heritage of Delhi continued to occupy high priority in the activities of the Government. Various courses in the field of Air Travel, Fare Air Ticketing, Cargo Services Management, Foreign Languages and Computer Application, etc., for providing technical and managerial trained manpower to the hospitality industry were conducted through the Delhi Chapter of IITTM. Delhi Tourism also organised various social, cultural and tourism festivals. Works has started on the construction of Netaji Subash Chandra Bose Memorial Tourist Complex at Tikri Kalan on National Highway -10 named as 'Azad Hind Gram'.

The Food Craft Institute continued to provide training in various discipline like cooking, bakery, reception, restaurant counter service, house keeping etc.

New Delhi Municipal Council (NDMC)

The New Delhi Municipal Council (NDMC) occupies a distinctive place in the set up of NCT of Delhi. Comprising an area of 42.74 square kilometers, NDMC caters to the municipal needs of the seat of the Union Government. The NDMC covers a population of 3.5 lakh and provides municipal service to about 12 lakh floating population. The Council has also undertaken various social, educational, cultural, entertainment and sports activities with a view to provide quality living. In order to provide improved services, replacement of 50 years old sewer and water lines are being executed. Through its 122 schools, NDMC is providing education from Nursery to Senior Secondary Level to the children of lower and middle-income group people.

Delhi police

Policing in Delhi is a daunting task specially in the context of Delhi's spiralling population, which an annual growth rate of more than half-a-million, of which around 40% lives in countless slum clusters. However, during the year under report, Delhi police stretched itself to the limit to enforce order and control crime. Some of its major achievements include:-

— Arrest of 14 persons responsible for causing bombs blasts in Delhi and adjoining areas (as many as 41 incidents of bomb explosions in Delhi and neighbouring States were solved with their arrest).

— Tracking down major terrorist operation with the arrest of a hardcore militant, Salim Junaid @ Abu Shahid along with his gang members from Hyderabad who had planned to replicate the Coimbatore blast of February 1998 in Hyderabad.

— Arrest of 43 militants, including 7 foreign nationals and 36 Indians and recovery of huge amount of

RDX, explosive powders, assorted firearms, hand grenades, detonators, etc., from them.

— Killing of dreaded criminals and extortionists such as Shiv Prakesh Shukla, Anju Pratap Singh and Sudhir Tripathi on September 22, 1998 and Bijender @ Birju on November 15, 1998, etc., in encounters.

— Successful rescue of several kidnapped persons from their abductors/ kidnappers

— Major crackdown on robber, in the wake of an alarming increase in the Capital, which resulted in arrest of 1169 persons and recovery of Rs.25 crores of looted property.

With a view to strengthening the field formation of Delhi Police, the Government sanctioned establishment of 17 additional Police Stations involving creation of 3100 posts at various levels and purchase of 126 vehicles, 140 wireless sets, arms and ammunitions, etc., at a recurring expenditure of Rs.25.01 crores per annum and a non-recurring expenditure of Rs.4.95 crores. It has also been decided to modernise the communication network by installation of state of the art UHF Digital Tracking Radio System at an expenditure of Rs. 14.21 crores to replace the conventional VHFs System which has limited operational capacity.

With a view to improving the quality of training facility for Delhi Police personnel, it has been decided to upgrade the Delhi Training School at Jharoda Kalan to a College with the most modern and state of the art training equipment and gadgets such as Computer Laboratory, Firing Simulators, Multi-Media Teaching Projector and Driving Simulators, etc.

A separate Anti-Extortions Cell has been set up under the Crime Branch of Delhi Police for effective handling the cases relating to extortion of money.

Pondicherry

The Union territory of Pondicherry, extending over an area of 492 sq.kms. has a population of 8.07 lakhs (Cemsus:1991). It comprises four regions, viz., Pondicherry, Karaikal, Mahe and Yanam with 5 municipalities and 10 community development blocks, consisting of 264 census villages.

Agriculture

Increase in productivity, diversification of cropping pattern and emphasis on horticultural crops continued to be the strategy for improving agricultural production in the territory. During the year 1998-99,40000 agricultural labourers were provided insurance cover. Paddy growers were given procurement bonus and framers were provided with subsidized organic manures.

Civil supplies

Essential commodities such as rice, wheat, sugar, palm oil, kerosene, etc., are being distributed through Public Distribution System to 2.51 lakh family ration card holders through a network of 392 fair shops. Effective steps were taken to identify the families below poverty line and 88851 cards were endorsed with red seal upto July 1998 enabling them to get 10 kilos of rice out of their total entitlement at a specially subsidised price.

Industries

During the year 1998-99, upto October 1998,93 new industrial units, including 10 medium scale and 3 large scale units, were registered in the territory. Industrial production registered a marked increase with total production worth Rs.4,90,565 lakhs by October 1998 as against production worth Rs.3,27,917 lakhs for the entire year 1997-98. Additional employment has been guaranteed for about 3000 persons during the year under report.

The District Industries Centre continued to provide training to educated unemployed youth and prospective entrepreneurs. An amount of Rs. 450 lakhs has been disbursed to the Pondicherry Industrial Promotion Development and Investment Corporation (PIPDIC) for setting up a Growth Centre at Polagam in Karaikal region at an estimated cost of Rs. 25 crores.

Health and family welfare

Health Service continued to be provided through a network of 8 hospitals, 453 primary health centres, 12 dispensaries and 3 chest clinics. Upto the end of October 1998,9350 children were immunised against polio and 16,620 children were given BCG vaccination. DTP was given to 9350 children during the period under report.

Water supply and sanitation

In order to improve water supply, 22 villages/habitations were taken up for augmentation work during the year 1998-99. Under Urban Water Supply Programme, augmentation of 3 zones out of 9 zones of urban areas have been completed and works is in progressing in zone III (Neelithope).

Education

Two colleges and 11 Senior Secondary have been established in the territory during the year under report. 87,525 students were given the benefit of free midday meals in primary schools.

Welfare

The Scheduled Castes, Scheduled Tribes, Backward classes and women were provided assistance under various welfare schemes. Old age pension was granted to 33,410 persons during the period upto October 1998.

6

National Security

More recently the exploitation of casteist and communal–religious sentiments for plainly electoral purposes in the Indian experience, has added a further dimension to the ethno-political sources of internal conflict. The strenght of the socio-economic causes underlying internal conflict might also be noted, arising largely from the spread of communications through a popular media like television to fan resentments among the under-privileged/deprived.

In the totality of its internal security problems during the eighties, India witnessed irridentist militancy in Kashmir and Punjab, ethnicity-related violent movements in its North-eastern states; Naxalite activity in Andhra Pradesh that has now spread to Maharashtra, Madhya Pradesh, Orissa and Bihar; LTTE-associated terrorism in Tamilnadu with similar incidents in other Southern states; regional agitations for Gorkhaland, Bodoland and Jharkand, that could encourage similar demands in Uttarakhand, Poorvanchal, Vidarha, Ladakh and Jammu; casteist violence embodied that is endemic to certain sensitive areas in the country but gained a national spread after demolition of the Babri Masjid.

There was an appreciable increase also in domestic law and order problems like riots for non-communal reasons, student and labour unrest, atrocities on women and scheduled categories of the population and so on.

An especial cause for violence has become the call to elections leading to great excitement that finds expression in clashes between the supporters of rival; candidates in the run-up to the elections, and in booth-capturing, prevention of electors reaching polling stations and so on, on election day. An incipient cause of tensions that would become more apparent in the years ahead would arise from rapid urbanisation in India. It is estimated to reach around 30% of the total population by the end of this century, but could reach between 35-40% in the more industrialised states. What is subsumed in these statistics is that around a third of the present urban population lives in slums, and their percentage could increase dramatically as a proportion of the total urban population. Civic servicers in urban areas, including the metropolitan centres, are already under great strain, with basic amenities like water, electricity, sewerage, roads, public transport and communication systems under tremendous strain. The concept of satellite townships has not shown much progress to arrest the ceaseless flow of rural population into the cities, primarily in search of employment. The ghettoisation of this largely itinerant, rootless and psychologically traumatised people living in appaling conditions, could lead to socio-economic tensions and conflicts in future.

The variegated and serious dimensions of the internal security threat to India in the coming years draws attention to the capability of the governance processes to overcome these challenges. The disconcerting situation obtaining is that the instrumentalities of the State, including its law and order apparatus, have suffered a deterioration in quality, but the problems of internal security are becoming more complex and acute. This has affected the basic functions of the State, which remains the maintenance of law and order, administration of justice, provision of communications facilities, and social services for the weaker sections of society. The machinery established for undertaking these various activities has uniformally been adversely affected.

Of interest to the seminal question of national/ internal security is the palpable decay in the efficience of the machinery for law and order and criminal justice administration. A large number of reasons like the politicisation of the bureaucracy and the police, the nexus established between organised crime and politics and communalism/casteism, institutional breakdown of the judicial system, and an all-too-eager recourse to deploying the armed forces to handle internal security problems that clearly lie within the competence of the existing police/para-military forces. The problems of governance revealed here draw attention to the growing weakness of the political parties and political institutions of Government that include both its legislative and administrative wings.

Defence

India's defence policy aims at promoting and sustaining durable peace in the sub-continent and equipping the defence forces adequately to safeguard aggression. The Supreme Command of the Armed Forces is vested in the President of India. The responsibility for national defence, however, rests with the Cabinet. The Defence Minister is responsible to Parliament for all matters concerning defence. Administrative and operational control of the armed forces is exercised by the Ministry of Defence and the three services headquarters.

Army

At the Army Headquarters in New Delhi, the Chief of the Army Staff is assisted by the Vice-Chief of the Army Staff and seven other Principal Staff Officers, namely, two Deputy Chiefs of the Army Staff, Adjtant General,

Quarter-Master General, Master General of Ordnance, Military Secretary and Engineer-in-Chief.

The Army is organised into five operational Commands, *viz.*, Southern, Eastern, Western, Central and Northern Command and one Training Command. Each Command is under a General Officer Commanding-in-Chief who holds the rank of Lieutenant General. General Officer Commanding-in-Chief commanding an operative command is the commander of demarcated geographical area and has both field and static formations under the command. The major field formations are Corps, Division and Brigade, commanded by a General Officer Commanding of the rank of Major General and Brigadier, respectively. The major static formations are Areas, independent Sub-Areas and Sub-Areas. An Area is commanded by a General Officer Commanding of the rank of Major General and an independent Sub-Area and Sub-Area by a Brigadier.

The Army consists of a number of arms and services. These are: Armoured Corps, Regiment of Artillery, Corps of Air Defence Artillery, Army Aviation Corps, Corps of Engineers, Corps of Signals, Mechanised Infantry, Infantry, Army Service Corps, Army Ordnance Corps, Corps of Electrical and Mechanical Engineers, Remount and Veterinary Corps, Military Police, Judge Advocate General Department, Army Physical Training Corps, Poineer Corps, Army Postal Service, Territorial Army, Defence Security Corps. In addition, the Army has its own Recruiting Organisation, Record Offices, Depots, Boys Establishments and Selection Centres and Training institutions.

Navy

The Navy responsible for defence and security of India's maritime interests and assests, both in times of war and peace. The Chief of the Naval Staff at the Naval

Headquarters, New Delhi, is assisted by four Principal Staff Officers, namely, the Vice Chief of Naval Staff, the Deputy Chief of Naval Staff, Chief of Personnel and Chief of Material.

The Navy has three commands *i.e.*, Western, Eastern and Southern with their headquarters located at Bombay, Visakhapatnam and Cochin respectively. Each Command is headed by a Flag Officer Commanding-in-Chief in the rank of Vice Admiral. Western Command and Eastern Command have under them operational fleets *i.e.*, Western and Eastern Fleets comprising warships, submarines, aircraft and other support ships. Southern Naval Command is responsible for all training activities of the Indian Navy.

The Indian Navy is a well balanced three dimensional force consisting of sophisticated missile capable warships, two aircraft carriers, minesweepers, advanced submarines and the latest aircraft in its inventory. Many of the warships are of indigenous design and have been constructed in Indian shipyards. These ships compare well with the ships of similar capability constructed by the advanced countries. The Naval forces are maintained and supported by modern dockyard facilities encompassing state-of-the art technology. At present, it has two major Naval bases at Bombay and Visakhapatnam.

Coast guard

The Coast Guard was constituted as an armed force of the Unin in 1978 under the Coast Guard Act, to protect the maritime and other national intersts in the maritime zones of India covering an area of approximately 28 lakh sq km. The force, which in headed by Director General Coast Guard is functioning under the effective control of the Ministry of Defence.

The headquarters of the force is presently located in New Dehli and regional headquaters are at Bombay, Mardras and Port Blair. The three regions, namely, Western, Eastern and Andaman and Nicobar cover 11 districts, one in each of the nine coastal states in the mainland and two in Andaman and Nicobar Islands. At present, the Coast Guard district headquarters are located at Porbandar in Gujarat, Bombay in Maharashtra, Vasco-da-Gama in Goa, New Mangalore in Karnataka and at Cochin in Kerala. Similary on the East coast, these are located at Madras in Tamil Nadu, Vizag in Andhra Pradesh, Paradeep in Orissa and Haldia in West Bengal. In addition independent Coast Guard stations are located at Vadinar, Okha, Tuticorin and Mandapam. Coast Guard air stations are in operation at Daman and Madras and Air Enclaves at Goa, Calcutta and Bombay. Establishment of stations at Kavaratti and Kamorta are being planned.

The force has effectively served national interests in high-risk areas. Foreign trawlers fishing illegally have been apprehended. Coast Guard ships and aircraft have been regularly assisting the customs authorities in anti-smuggling operations. Besides, the force is available for search and rescue operations, anti-pollution and other duties in the maritime zones of the country. The recent oil spill situations off Andaman and Nicobar and Goa were efficiently handled by the Coast Guard.

Air force

The Air Forse is organised both on functional as well as geographical basis. There are five operational commands. These are: Western Air Command, South-Western Air Command, Central Air Command, Eastern Air Command and Southern Air Command. In addition, Maintenance Command and Training Command are two functional commands.

At the Air Headquarters in New Delhi, the Chief of the Air Staff is assisted by the Vice-Chief of Air Staff, Deputy Chief of Air Staff, Air Officer Incharge Personnel, Air Officer Incharge Administration, Air Officer Incharge Maintenance and Inspector General (Flight Safety and Inspection). Each of these six Principal Staff Officers is assisted by an Assistant Chief of the Air Staff.

Today, the Air Force has an array of modern aircraft on its inventory besides other hi-tech electronic and support equipment. The aircraft fleet consists of fighter bombers, air superiority fighters, interceptors, transport and logistic aircraft and helicopters. The fighters force comprises *MiG-21* variants, *MiG-23s, MiG-25s, MiG-27s* and *Jaguars* which represent the modern generation strike aircraft. Older generation aircraft like the *Hunters* and *Canberras* are presently used in training and ancillary roles. *MiG-29s* and *Mirage-2000s* are air defence aircraft of the present generation. The transport fleet consists of *IL-76s, AN-32s,* the indigenously produced *HS-748s, Dornier-228* which are manufactured under licence by HAL and *Boeing 737s* which are used for VIP duties. While the *IL-76s* provides the Air Force with heavylift and strategic capabilities, *AN-32s* and *HS-748s* are also used in training role besides performing air maintenance and communication duties. The helicopter fleet consists of *Chetak, Cheetah, MI-8, MI-17* and the heavy-lift *MI-26* which is the largest helicopter in the world. All these aircraft are used for high altitude operations and provide logistics support to our ground forces. *Chetak/Cheetah* helicopters maufactured by HAL for the Air Force, are also used as Anti-Tank Guided Missile (ATGM) carriers, air borne Forward Air Controller (FAC) and for search and rescue operations. *MI-8* helicopters are specially modified to undertake tasks in Antarctica. In addition, the force has been supplemented with *MI-25* which performed yeoman service for the IPKF in Sri Lanka and

MI-35 attack helicopters. *HPT-32* and *HJT-16 Kiran,* both manufactured by HAL are used as basic and applied stage trainers respectively with the *Kiran* being supplemented by Polish *Iskara* aircraft. A landmark in the IAD was the commissioning of the first batch of women pilots on 17 December 1994. These pilots are now serving in front line transport Squadrons. The next batch women pilots is currently undergoing helicopter training and all have achieved solo flight status on *Chetak* and *Cheetah* helicopters.

The army

As for the Army, the project plans centred around the 155 mm Bofors guns were completely neutralised for reasons well known. In the process the ambitious programme of manufacturing about 1000 field Howitzers aided by technology transfer from Sweden for manufacture of ammunition got stalled. Worse still the Army's urgent requirements of the self-propelled guns of the same calibre got stuck up.

In Spite of the tumult over its acquisition, the 400 odd Swedish Howitzers played a decisive role in both the north-west as well as the north-east borders. Pakistan's repeated attempts togain a foothold in the Siachen Glacier were foiled by the Army's timely deployment and effective use of the Bofors guns.

So too, in the eastern sector, the advent of the 155 mm guns and their potential for long range bombardment in the himalayan heights put the Chinese in check and there were no more intrusions like the one in Arunachal Pradesh in the late 80's.

It would not be out of place to mention that the Indian Army has been involved in the arduous task of neutralising insurgencies in the entire North-East during the last 50 years. Neighbouring countries like China, Burma and the then East Pakistan (Bangaldesh) evinced more than usual interest in provoking various insurgent and ethnic groups in a bid to destabilise the country and bleed our defence forces.

The Indian Army nonetheless tackled the situation with minimum force required and to a large extent has succeeded in winning the sympathy of the people through various aid to civilian population. More than two division of troops had to be deployed and kept on alert to foil underground insurgencies aided and abetted by hostile countries. In fact, this became part of our defence preparedness plans and specialised units and training centres had to be raised.

To relieve the troops from being locked in such insurgency situatons and policing roles, the Rashtriya Rifles has been established. Forty Batallions have now taken up positions in such conflict situations. The Army will concentrate on its primary role to keep fit and trained to face any eventuality from across the borders. In addition, the BSF and Assam Rifles are there to assist the armed forces.

The navy

Although the Navy has been slightly better off with its own naval design Bureau and a home shipping industry, the lack of funds has slowed down the pace of construction of new warships. On this score one cannot fault the Navy for lack of planning. It is more in the sphere of implementation. Yet both government and shipyards have to be congratulated for additions, especially in the field of Corvettes, Missile Boats and Submarine, two of which were built at Mazagon Docks, Bombay. There is an ongoing project for the construction of three destoyers of 6000 tonnes each beginning with the Delhi, Mysore and Mumbai. Three advanced and modified versions of the Godavari class are under construction at the Garden Reach Workshop, Calcutta and the first 'Brahmaputra' has already been launched.

The demand is there for more subs, both of the Kilo and the German Hunter class but government is yet to take a decisison. Fortunately the cash crunch has not affected the progressive addition of Sea Harriers with the Navy but they require an additional platform in time, since Vikrant has already been virtually decommissioned. The life of aircraft carier Viraat is also getting shorter by the Years. Fortunately, both the nodel Ministry and the Navy is in the process of acquiring a sea control ship, possibly from Russia. As a long term option, India of course has the potential to build its own Aircraft Carrier at Cochin shipyard.

The Navy with its spreading blue water capability has no doubt created an impact on neighbouring countries, especially in the East and even caused a sense of alarm in far away Australia which has however with the passage of time been convinced that India has no expansionist intentions except to guard its coastline particularly its Exclusive Economic Zone and Oil Installations on the high seas.

The Indian Navy has also raised the 'Marine Commando Force', a specialised unit which can operate in various under water and off-shore areas. India is the second country after the USA to build up this highly mobile and potent naval commando force. During the operations in Sri Lanka, the Marine Commando Force won laurels and proved its worth as a deterrent to the enemy.

The air force

The maintsay of the Air Force has been the MIG fleet ranging from MIG-21 to MIG-29, supplemented by the Jaguars and the Mirage-2000. It goes the credit of the Air

Force that it showed its capabilities in combined operations first in 1971 and some 20 years later in the Maldives. In 1971, the Air Force was ready to take on the task of dropping a para batallion over Tangail to deliver a deadly psychological blow that hastened the surrender of Pakistani forces in Bangaldesh. Such airborne operations had become imperative due to a threat posed by an American Carrier group heading towards Chittagong. It would not be out of place to mention that the press played the role of a force multiplier. A foreign news agency reported that a para brigade had been dropped on the outskirts of Dacca and that did the trick.

But more outstanding was the reflex action response of the Air Force in fulfilling the requirement of the maldives President Abdul Gayoom in meeting a coup attempt by foreign mercenaries against his democratically elected government. In less than six hours, the Air Force with its giant IL-76 had landed Indian troops in and around Male, the Maldivian Capital and foiled the coup attempt. In this operation, the Air Force displayed its combat and communication capabilities across the Indian ocean and this was indeed an eye opener for Western Powers. Not only this, it was a snub for Pakistan as its offer for help was rejected by the Maldivian President.

Fortunately, for the Air Force, it has also a large manufacturing and overhauling base with rich experience in the production and maintenance of almost the entire MIG fleet and Jaguars. It is against this background that these facilities will not only be upgraded but considerably augmented by the project for modernisation of the MIG-21 BIS fleet of 125 fighters. Two prototypes of the upgraded MIG-21 BIS are expected shortly and the HAL will undertake the fabrication of the updated versions. This programme is expected to be completed in less than two years and should amply make up for repeated delays in the LCA project. The air defence of the country would be well secured with the new look MIG-21 BIS fleet, which will be equipped with four times higher fire power against ground targets and would be an even match for F-16 in service with Pak Air Force.

The acquisition of the Sukhoi-30 culminates a long wait by the Air Force, which had spelt out its requirements for this multi-role air superiority fighter far back in 1990. For the first time perhaps India has gone for a new weapon system not merely based on the Pakistan syndrome but with much wider perspective that will cover portions of China, Myanmar and South-East Asia. In addition, the regional security requirements will be amply met by the longer range and sweep of the Sukhois which could neutralise any hostile activity emanating from countries in the neighbourhood like Iran, Afghanistan and even possibly Central Asian States. It will be pertinent to point out in this context that Sukhois will have mid air refuelling capability. India has signed a contract with Russia for 40 Sukhois and significantly this includes the transfer of technology and indigenous manufacture of this multi-role fighter planes. For the first time the Russion agencies have agreed to permit DRDO to participate in R & D and joint development of avoinics of the aircraft.

Commissioned ranks

Following are the commissioned ranks in the three services; each rank is shown opposite to its equivalent in the other service:

Recruitment

The Armed Forces symbolise the unity of the country and the ideals of national integration. Recruitment to the Armed Forces is open to all Indian nationals, irrespective of caste, creed, community, religion and region. The endeavour has been to provide free and equal opportunities to all sections of the population to join the Armed Forces and render service in accordance with the ideals of secularism, democracy and social justice. India's Armed Forces offer challenging openings to our youth. A remarkable feature of recruitment to the Armed Forces is that it is entirely voluntary. The competition for entry into the service is intense, reflective of the increasing numbers of educated youth in the country, coupled with the attractive terms and conditions of service, and the high level of respect commanded by the Armed Forces. Recruitment is made from different states/union territories on the basis of their recruitable male population. Conscious efforts are made to take care of the special needs of the border areas and hilly and other remote areas, by lowering educational and certain other criteria to suit their requirements.

Induction of women into the armed forces

While provision has all along existed for women to join the Armed Forces Medical Services, the Armed Forces Dental Services and the Military Nursing Service, Section 12 of the Army Act provided that women would not normally be eligible for enrolment in the Army. Similar provisions also existed in the cases of the Air Force and the Navy. However, in acknowledgment of the changing times, the Government has approved the induction of women into selected non-combatant branches in the three Forces. The entry of women has however, been restricted to the Officer Cadres, and they are on Short Service Commission basis. Further continuance of schemes would be decided on the basis of the experience gained. In pursance of this decision, several women officers have since joined the Service, in the EME, Signals, Engineers, Army Education Corps, Army Ordnance Corps, Army Service Corps and in the Judge Advocate General Department.

Recruitment of commissioned officers

Entry to the Officer Cadres in the Armed Forces is primarily through the Union Public Service Commission (UPSC). Graduates are eligible to join the Armed Forces through an examination known as the Combined Defence Services Examination (CDSE) conducted by the UPSC twice a year. Candidates who quality in the examination join the Indian Military Academy (IMA), the Air Force Academy and the Naval Academy for pre-commission training. Individuals selected for Short Service Commission are trained at the Officers Training Academy. The candidates seeking a career in the Armed Forces after completion of 10+2 general education join the National Defence Academy (NDA). UPSC holds the entrance examination twice a year for entry in the NDA. They join the respective Service Academies *viz.* the Indian Military Academy (IMA) for the Army, the Air Force Academy for the Air Force and the Naval Academy for the Navy, for their pre-commission training.

There is also direct entry of officers through the Service Selection Boards (SSBs) for the Army and Navy, and through the Air Force Selection Board for the Air Force, without any written examination by the UPSC. Candidates in the age group of 20 to 27 years with Engineering Degree and Post-Graduates in specified subject in the age group of 23 to 27 years are eligible for interview by the respective Selection Boards of the following branches of the Armed Forces: Armed Engineers, Electrical and Mechanical Engineering, Signals, Army Education Corps, Military Farms, Remount and Veterinary Corps: Navy–Electrical and Engineering, Engineering (Naval Architects) Logistics, Law, Education, Air Traffic control: Air Force–Aeronautic Engineers (Electronics), Aeronautic Engineers (Mechanical), Administration, Education, Logistics, Accounts, Meteorology.

In July 1992, the Government approved a University Entry Scheme, initially for a period of three years, for induction of Engineering students in their final year/pre-final into the Army. This scheme is already operating in the Air Force and the Navy. Engineering students of various disciplines studying in the final/pre-final years in recognised universities/institutions are eligible for induction into the technical branches/services of the Army as short service commissioned officers with the rank of Second Lieutenants under this scheme. Their salary, however, is paid in one lump sum on their joining the IMA for training on the successful completion of which they will be granted permanent commission in the Army. An intake of 100 officers per year has been planned under this scheme.

With a view to mitigate the shortage of Technical Officers (Engineering) in the Army, the Government also approved a short service commission (Tech) Entry Scheme. This envisages recruitment of qualified technical graduates through the SSBs and their enrolment in the Officers' Training Academy (OTA), Madras after medical tests for a ten month course. At the end of the course, the successful candidates will receive short service commission. Thereafter, they will be governed by the rules applicable to the other short service commissioned officers.

Recruitment of medical officers in the Armed Forces is done through two sources. All MBBS graduates passing out from the Armed Forces Medical College, Pune are granted Permanent Commission. Apart from this, post graduates/MBBS degree holders passing out from civilian medical colleges are selected through competitive examinations, on an all-India basis, conducted by the Directorate General of Armed Forces, partyly for grant of Regular Commission and partly for grant of Short Service Commission.

Research and development

Defence Research and Development Organisation (DRDO) was established in 1958 by amalgamating Defence Science Organisation and some of the technical development establishments. A separate Department of Defence Research and Development was formed in 1980 which operates through network of 50 laboratories/establishments. The Department is engaged in the pursuit of self-reliance in critical technologies of relevance to national security. It formulates and executes programmes of scientific research, design and development leading to induction of state-of-the-art weapons, platforms and other equipments required by the Armed Forces. It functions under the control of Scientific Adviser to *Raksha Mantri* who is also Secretary, Defence Research and Development.

Research and development activities of the Department cover important demarcated disciplines like aeronatuics, rockets and missiles, electronics and instrumentation, combat vehicles, engineering systems, naval systems, armament technology including explosives research, system sciences including advanced computing, high altitude agriculture, physiology, food technology, nuclear medicine and allied sciences. In addition, the Department also assists the Services by rendering technical advice regarding formulation of requirements, evaluation of systems to be acquired, fire and explosive safety and mathematical/statistical analysis of operational problems.

The notable development successes of the Department include flight stimulators for aircraft, light field gun, 5.56 mm rifle, charge line mine clearing system for safe passage of vehicles in the battlefield, illuminating ammunition for enhancing night fighting capabilities, cluster weapons system for fighter aircraft, naval mines and new generation bombs for high speed aircraft and low-level bombing. Different radars like low-level tracking radar *Indra-I* and *Indra-II* for Army and Air Force, light weight field artillery radar, battlefield surveillance radar, secondary surveillance radar hae been developed. Bridge Layer Tank-*Kartik,* military bridging system, advanced ship sonar systems, advance sonobuoy, naval decoys, naval simulators, torpedo launchers, advanced materials and composites for military applications are also some of the other achievements of the Department.

The main battle tank *Arjun* having superior fire power, high mobility and excellent protection has been successfully developed. Army has accepted the tank for induction in Service and the tank is now under troop trails in actual field conditions. Simultaneously, planning action has been initiated by Department of Defence Production and Supplies for productionisation of *MBT Arjun.* A Light Combat Aircraft (LCA) is under hardware fabrication and engineering stage and integration of some of the sub-assemblies has already commended. An advanced technology gas turbine engine *GTX-35VS* named *Kaveri* for use in LCA is under development under a separate programme. Integrated Guided Missile Development Programme (IGMDP) comprises four missile system, namely, *Prithvi,* surface-to-surface tactical battlefield missile; *Akash,* medium range surface-to-air missile; *Trishul,* short range surface-to-air missile; and *Nag,* third generation anti-tank missile. The programme also included development of a re-entry technology demonstrator project called *Agni.*

The other major programmes which are in advanced stage of development/productionisation are: Pilotless Target Aircraft (PTA), Composite Sonar and Tactical Weapon Control System-*'Panchendriya'* for Navy, LMG and carbine in 5.56 mm calibre and multi-barrel rocket launching system-*'Pinaka'.* A Marine Acoustic Research

Ship-'*Sagardhwani*' has been designed and built indigenously. The ship is one of the most modern research. A PACE-PLUS parallel processing computer, configured with advanced commercially available micro-processors as computing nodes, has been designed and developed.

The Department has also rendered assistance to para-military and police agencies by way of supply of bullet proof vehicles, bullet proof vests, amenity vehicles, such as kitchen lorry, communication equipment, water pressure jet based anti-riot vehicles and several other types of equipments. The Department also offers specialised training at its two primier training institutions.

Production and supplies

A substantial part of defence stores needed by the Services is now being developed and produced within the country. The responsibility for this has been entrusted to the Department of Defence Production and Supplies in the Ministry of Defence. The Department directs and coordinates production of material and equipment required by the Armed Forces.

Ordnance factories

At present, 39 ordnance factories spread all over India operate a wide-range of technologies and product mix. Some of the important products are field guns, anti-aircraft guns, mortars, various small arms and ammunition for weapons and guns, rockets, projectiles, pyro-technics, bombs, grenades, mines, demolition charges, depth charges, infantry combat vehicles, battle tanks, self-propelled guns, transport trucks and petrol vehicles, high-altitude and combat clothing, optical and fire control instruments, engineering equipment, supply dropping equipmet including parachutes, rubberised items, various knitted and woven items like blankets, web equipment and a wide range of general stores are produced by them. Production of 5.56 mm (indigenously designed) weapon system has started in ordnance factories. These factories are also producing bombs required by Air Force. Besides, liquid fuel required for successful flight trials of *Prithvi* and *Agni* missiles, igniters and copper liners for the warheads were also supplied in the development of *Prithvi* missile. The production of *Ajeya tank (T-72), Sarath (BMP-II),* infantry combat vehicle are carried out at Heavy Vehicle Factory, Avadi and Ordnance Factory, Medak, respectively. A sophisticated opto-electronic production unit has been set up at Dehra Dun to produce the opto-electronic fire control and night vision devices required for *Ajeya Tank (T-72-MI* and *Sarath* infantry combat vehicle is planned from 1994-95. To utilise the sparable capacities, after meeting the services requirements, linear and lateral shift in customer product profiles has been taken up as a major thrust area of operations.

Jonga for civil market

As a part of diversification efforts, Vehicles Factory, Jabalpur (VFJ) has taken up modification and upgradation of Jonga. The vehicle, conforming to military standards, is not only sturdy but also has a very high pick up, high fuel efficiency of 16 km per litre (under test conditions) and a maximum speed of 120 kmph with gradient climbing capability of one in three. It has been decided to launch Jonga in the civil open market. VFJ has a captive capacity to manufacture 20,000 Jonga per annum. Out of this, 10,000 vehicles are to be released in the civil market and remaining 10,000 are reserved for the Army and exports.

Defence undertakings

There are eight public sector undertakings (PSUs) under the Department of Defence Production and Suppliers.

These are: Hindustan Aeronautics Limited (HAL), Bharat Electronics Limited (BEL), Bharat Earth Movers rail coaches, track laying equipments, heavy duty trucks, trailers, diesel engines etc. BEML is a leader in earth-moving industry with over 70 per cent market share. Its equipments and systems are productively deployed in India and over 30 other countries across the globe.

Mazagon Dock Limited (MDL) is the country's leading shipbuilding yard and can build warships up to 6,000 DWT displacement and merchant ships up to 27,000 DWT. It has units at Bombay, Nhava and Mangalore and headquarters at Bombay. At present, its major activities include construction of sub-marines, missile-boats and destroyers etc., for the Indian Navy and off-shore supply vessels and well-head platforms etc., for the Oil and Natural Gas Commission (ONGC). The company also provides diving services as well as services for coating/laying sub-sea pipes.

Garden Reach Shipbuilders and Engineers Limited (GRSE) is a multi-unit shipyard-cum-general engineering company. It has six units in and around Calcutta and a Diesel Engine Plant at Ranchi (Bihar). Its corporate office is at Calcutta. It has three distinct divisions, namely, ship, engineering and engine divisions. It is presently engaged in the construction of war ships and auxiliary vessels of various types for the Navy and the Coast Guard and to undertake repair of vessels of these two organisations. Other products of the company include a variety of high technology ship-borne equipments, portable Bailey type steel bridges, marines sewage treatment plant, dock-machinery items, turbine pumps for the agricultural sector, diesel engines, etc.

The activities of Goa Shipyards Limited (GSL) located at Vasco-da-Gama, primarily comprise construction and repair-reit of ships/vessels. It has undertaken construction/refit of variety of vessels for the Indian Navy and the Coast Guard as well as for the non-defence sector. It is currently building advanced off-shore patrol vessels of in-house design.

Bharat Dynamics Limited (BDL), established in 1970, is primarily engaged in the manufacture of guided missiles and allied equipments. It has units at Hyderabad and Bhanur Medak district. Its corporate office is at Hyderabad. It is also the prime production agency for manufacture of four new missile systems, namely, *Prithvi, Trishul, Akash and Nag*, being developed indigenously. Its activities which had earlier been diversified into a number of Naval projects now proposes to take up manufacture of small arms required for para-military forces of the country.

Mishra Dhatu Nigam Limited (MIDHANI) located at Hyderabad was incorporated in 1973. MIDHANI's product range includes super alloys, maraging steels, heat resistance alloys, controlled expansion alloys, tungsten, molybednum etc., in variety of mill forms.

Resettlement and welfare of ex-servicemen

In order to maintain a youthful profile of the Armed Forces, over 55,000 service personnel are retired/released every year at a comparatively young age. Majority of service personnel at the time of retirement are at an age where they have numerous unfinished responsibilities which necessitate their taking up of a second career. The Government is seized of this problem of rehabilitating them through provision of employment in organised sector or through self-employment. The welfare of ex-servicemen has been accepted as a national responsibility.

The Directorate General of Resettlement (DGR) under the Ministry of Defence (MOD) has been set up to look after all matters connected with resettlement and welfare of ex-servicemen and their dependents. A Kendriya Sainik Board under the Chairmanship of *Raksha Mantri* has been established for laying down general policy for the welfare of ex-servicemen and their dependents, for the administration of welfare funds, and also for coordinating the work of the Sainik Boards in the country. At the state level, the Rajya Sainik Boards, and at the district level the Zila Sainik Boards, have been established. The Government of India bears 50 per cent of the expenditure incurred on the organisations of Rajya and Zila Sainik Boards, the remaining expenditure is borne by the respective state governments.

Resettlement

Resettlement activities for the retired/retiring service personnel consist of the following: (a) training programmes to reorient retiring Defence personnel towards civil emploment; (b) providing re-employment opportunities in government/semi-government/public sector organisations and (c) schemes for self-employment.

In order to equip retiring service personnel for employment, suitable training programmes have been devised. They equip them for employment in civil organisations and for self-employment. For retiring service officers, the following training programmes were introduced during 1994-95: (a) Diploma in Industrial Security and Labour Laws; (b) Coaching for Air Line Transport Pilot Licence/Senior Commercial Pilot Licence/Commercial Helicopter Pilot Licence; (c) Consultant in ISO-9000; (d) Quality Assurance Manager ISO-9000 and (e) Deputy Quality Assurance Manager ISO-9000. Up to March 1995, 882 officers were trained. The vocational training, ITI training and on the job training are presently being conducted for retiring Service personnel other than officers.

Re-employment

Re-employment constitutes a major means of rehabilitation of ex-servicemen. To achieve this goal both the Central and state governments have provided various concessions/facilities. These include reservation of posts, relaxations in age/educational standards, priority in employment etc. The Central Government has reserved 10 per cent of Group 'C' and 20 per cent of Group 'D' posts for ex-servicemen in Central ministries/ departments. The percentage of reservation in public sector undertakings and nationalised banks in these are 14½ and 24½ per cent respectively. Besides, there is 10 per cent reservation for the post of Assistant Commandants in para-military Forces. Reservation under the state governments varies from two per cent to 20 per cent. There is no reservation for ex-servicemen in Bihar, Kerala and Megahalaya.

DGR has been nominating ex-servicemen security agencies to various PSUs and private sector organisations. These security agencies provide employment opportunities for officers and other ranks. There are over 173 ex-servicemen security agencies which are registered with DGR, of which 130 have been sponsored for work. This alone has generated employment opportunities for over 6,419 ex-servicemen and over 250 officers.

There is considerable scope for absorption of ex-servicemen in para-military forces like CRPF, BSF, ITBP, CISF, etc. However, the response of ex-servicemen for joining these forces has been generally poor. With a view to achieve fuller utilisation of reserved vacancies, special recruitment rallies were organised in selected states. During 1993, special recruitment drives were conducted by CISF.

The concept of Ecological Task Force was mooted in

1992 for the purpose of restoring the forest cover in regions where significant deforestation had taken place. These units were initially raised in three states *viz.*, Uttar Prasdesh, Rajasthan and J&K. The task forces are manned by ex-servicemen who are paid salaries as per TA scales. Every individual, irrespective of his rank prior to retirement, is re-employed as a sepoy. Ministry of Defence provides officers to command these units.

Schemes for self-employment

Important schemes for self employment for ex-servicemen are SEMFEX-I, SEMFEX-II and SEMFEX-III. These schemes have been launched in collaboration with the Small Industries Development Bank of India, NABARD and the Khadi and Village Industries Commission for providing extensive self-employment opportunities for ex-servicemen and their dependents.

The SEMFEX-I Scheme was launched in April, 1987. Under this Scheme, financial assistance is provided to ex-servicemen to set up small industrial projects for self-employment. Loans under this Scheme are provided by the respective State Financial Corporation. As on 31 December 1994 there were 6,686 beneficiaries and the amount sanctioned is to the tune of Rs. 179.27 crore since inception.

The SEMFEX-II Scheme was launched in January 1988 by the DGR in collaboration with the National Bank for Agricultural and Rural Development (NABARD) to provide assistance for agricultural and allied activities. Under the Scheme, financial assistance up to Rs. 7.5 lakh for setting up of industrial units/service establishments is given. The ceiling of Rs. 7.5 lakh is, however, not applicable for setting up of units relating to agro-industries. Since inception and up to December 1994 loans amounting to Rs. 12.30 crore have been sanctioned to 2,352 beneficiaries.

The SEMFEX-III Scheme was launched in October 1991 in collaboration with the Khadi and Village Industries Commission (KVIC). It provides self employment opportunities for setting up village industries under the purview of KVIC. Under this Scheme, ex-servicemen and their widows are eligible to take up self-employment ventures. Financial assistance for such ventures is provided under a liberalised pattern of assistance by the KVIC. The loans granted to village industries under this Scheme carry a rate of interest of four per cent and there is no interest on loan for *Khadi* units. The Scheme is picking up. Up to December 1994, a loan of Rs. 1.42 crore was sanctioned in 188 cases.

Schemes have also been launched in collaboration with Bombay Mercantile Cooperative Bank and Oriental Bank of Commerce to provide financial assistance to ex-servicemen and their widows on easy terms. In addition to the above schemes for financial assistance, certain other measures have also been taken to assist ex-servicemen in their self employment ventures. These are: (a) Allotment of sheds/plots; (b) Price subsidy to ex-servicemen units; (c) Allotment of surplus class V-B vehicles; (d) Allotment of repairable typewriters and duplicators; (e) Transportation of bulk LPG; (f) Allotment of Mother Dairy milk booths, fruit and vegetable outlets; (g) Transportation of coal and (h) Allotment of petroleum product agencies.

Welfare

Before April, 1993 there were four separate funds *viz.*, amalgamated Special Fund for War Bereaved, War Disabled and other ex-Servicemen/serving personnel; (i) Flag Day Fund; (ii) ST Dunstan's (India) and KSB Fund and (iv) Indian Gorkha Ex-Servicemen's Welfare Fund. These separate funds have been merged into an 'Armed Forces Flag Day Fund'.

The Kendriya Sainik Board (KSB) administers 'Armed Forces Flag Day Fund' for the welfare and rehabilitation of ex-servicemen, war widows, disabled service personnel and their dependents. The total corpus of the fund, as on 31 March 1995 was Rs. 45.60 crore. The corpus of the fund is invested with Banks/PSUs. The income accruing from interest is utilised for the various welfare activities. In the year 1994-95, Rs. 2.20 crore were spent on the major welfare activities. Financial assistance is also provided to institutions such as Paraplegic Homes at Kirkee and Mohali, Cheshire Homes, Military Hospitals, St. Dunstan After Care Organisations and Homes for taking care or old and physically handicapped ex-servicemen and their dependents. Financial assistance is also provided to individual ex-servicemen suffering from serious diseases for treatment in civil hospitals in case they cannot be treated in Military Hospitals and have not availed similar assistance from any other source. During 1994-95, a sum of Rs. 20,59,719.60 was sanctioned for the treatment of serious diseases.

Census of ex-servicemen/widows

To collect reliable data about ex-servicemen/widows population and update it on a regular basis a census of ex-servicemen is being carried out by DGR through Zila Sainik Boards (ZSBs) with effect from 15 May 1992. The Scheme envisages registration of retired defence service personnel with their ZSBs and issue of I-cards to the eligible ex-servicemen/widows. As per the feedback received, a total of 12.01 lakh ex-servicemen and 2.06 lakh widows have been registered and were reported to be surviving as on 31 December 1994.

Concessions to ex-servicemen

The Government has been granting various concessions to ex-servicemen from time to time. The major concessions granted to different categories of personnel or their dependents cover assistance in the field of education, reservation for wards in professional institutions, reservations in Sainik Schools and Military Schools, medical treatment, assistance for construction/ repair of houses, financial assistance for the marriage of daughters, canteen facilities, rail and air travel concessions. Besides, financial assistance from the Raksha Mantri's Discretionary Fund (RMDF) is given to old and infirm exservicemen and to their widows in indegent circumstances.

The revised rates of financial assistance are: (a) Assistance to old infirm ex-servicemen/widows of ex-servicemen Rs. 250 per month for two years; (b) Marriage of daughters of ex-servicemen/widows in penury Rs. 4000; (c) Repair of house for ex-servicemen/widows in penury Rs. 5,000; (d) Medical treatment-depending upon the nature and gravity of ailment subject to a maximum of Rs. 8,000; (e) Education of children of ex-servicemen/ widows in penury Rs. 35 per month per child for up to three children up to class X and (f) Other cases in respect of ex-servicemen/widows in penury (like natural calamities, accidental death or where RM/RRM feel that the case deserves sysmpathetic consideration–no single transaction to exceed Rs. 8,000.

Inter-ministerial committee

In pursuance of the recommendation of the high level empowered committee headed by the *Raksha Mantri* on improvement in the retirement pensions of Defence Personnel, the Ministry of Defence constituted an Inter-Ministerial Committee to deal with the problems of ex-servicemen other than those relating to pensionary matters. Accordingly, a committe under the chairman-ship of an Additional Secretary in the Ministry of Defence was set up. This committee included representatives from the Ministry of Finance, Ministry of

Law, Department of Pension and Pension and Pensioners' Welfare and other relevant organisations. The Committee considered 53 demands of ex-servcemen. It has recommended/partly recommended 33 demands, noted that five demands were not found justified. The demands which have already been accepted by Government are: (i) Permission for commercial employment after retirement; (ii) Provision of Soft Seed Capital Assistance under SEMFEX-II Scheme; (iii) Non-allotment of oil production agencies to ex-servicemen/widows; (iv) Reservation in purchase from ex-servicemen entrepreneurs; and (v) Issue of Last Pay Certificate along with discharge certificate.

Recruitment of other ranks in army and sailors in navy

There are 12 Zonal Recruiting Officers (ZROs) and 58 Branch Recruiting Officers (BROs) spreasd throughout the country. In addition, there is an Independent Recruiting Office (IRO) at Delhi. In order to inform the potential candidates well in advance of the commencement of recruitment extensive recruitment publicity is undertaken throughout the country, including in remote areas. Recruitment rules provide for relaxation in respect of educational and physical standards to the candidates from certain specified backward, remote and tribal regions to give them due representation in the Army. Relaxation in physical standards is also given to one son and one grandson of serving soldiers, ex-servicemen, widows of battle casualties, etc. The recruitment to the Navy has been clubbed with Army from the beginning. The recruitment demand is projected to Army Headquarters by Naval Headquarters.

Airmen

Recruitment of Airmen to the Indian Air Force is done through the Central Airmen Selection Board located at the Air Force Station, New Delhi. There are 13 selection centres under this Board and they make the necessary arrangements for the conduct of selection tests and final enrolment. After seeking the application through advertisements in national/regional dailies and through the mass media, a written test on an all-India basis is held and the all India merit list is drawn up with help of computers.

A Pilot Project has been undertaken for the direct recruitment of trained manpower from the civil stream in the trades, such as clerks, drives, and Surveyor Automated Cartography. Besides direct recruitment of technically qualified civilian personnel as JCO (Catering) has been introduced.

National cadet corps

The National Cadet Corps (NCC) has emerged as the single largest structured youth movement in India. It was established on 15 July 1948. It has 11.5 lakh boys and girls in the Senior and Junior Divisions in the Army, Navy and Air Force Wings. This strength covers four per cent of the eligible student population in the country. NCC with motto 'Unity and Discipline' has following aims: (a) to develop qualities of character, courage, comradeship, leadership, secular outlook, spirit of adventure and sportsmanship and the ideal of selfless service among the youth to make them useful citizens; and (b) to create a human resource of organised, trained and motivated youth, to provide leadership in all walks of life including the Armed Forces and to be always available for the service of the nation.

Director General NCC located at New Delhi controls and oversees various activities of the NCC through 16 NCC Directorates spread across the country. There is a Central Advisory Committee for the NCC to provide overall policy guidelines. NCC is manned by Service personnel, whole time NCC officers and civilians. One lecturer/teacher in each educational institution is appointed as Associate NCC Officer.

During 1994-95, 21 centrally organised camps were held in which 5,575 cadets participated from Army, Navy, and Air and Girls Wings and 66 National Integration Camps were conducted across the country in which nearly 35,185 cadels have participated. A total of 3,65,151 cadets have attended Annual Training Camps till March 1995. One hundred and sixty girl cadets attached with Air Units attended the ATC at Belgaum and 160 girls attached with Naval Units attended ATC at Visakhapatam. As many as 110 officers and 8,902 cadets participated in attachment training during the year, 853 girl cadets did attachment training with Armed Forces hospitals. Twenty boys and 20 girls did para basic courses at Agra during November-December 1994. Besides, 4,59,992 NCC cadets participated in social service activities such as blood donation, eye donation, Cheshire homes, anti-dowry pledge, adult education etc., and 6,45,369 saplings were planted.

A team of eight officers and 42 cadets (21 boys and 21 girls) visited Canada in July 1994 under Indo-Canada Youth Exchange Programme. A similarly composed Canadian contingent was in India till January 1995. While 57 cadets visited other foreign countries on a reciprocal Youth Exchange Programme and one officer from Singapore and 32 foreign cadets from seven countries attended the Republic Day Camp (NCC) 1995. During 1994-95, 48 NCC personnel were awarded DGNCC's Commendation Cards with badges for outstanding contribution to the organisation.

Great achievments

In talking of operational capability, one must remember with pride, the magnificent contribution by our network of Ordnance Factories which produce almost every weapons system and ammunition used by the three services. What is needed now is a large—scale induction of the latest technology from abroad to meet the specific requirements of the latest acquisitions in the three services. Equally in place is the well deserved tribute to the vast Research and Development activities under the umbrella of DRDO. No doubt, the latest INSAS Rifles systems may have its drawbacks, but as has been rightly pointed out by Ordnance experts there is imperative need for acquiring requisite technology from abroad for improving its design since such guns are already in use in USA and Austria.

India can be proud of its IMDP (Integrated Missile Development Programme) which has now after more than two decades produced four missiles with varied applications-Prithvi, Akash, Trishul and Nag. This family meets the requirements of multifaceted attack and defensive modes. But the crowing glory of defence research has been its development of the Intermediate Range Balistic Missile, the Agni with its range upto 2500, depending on the load.

The entire missile programme barring the Agni, is on the threshold of the production stage and it is here in this context that the defence sector undertakings such as Bharat Dynamics, the nodal agency, the HAL, Bharat Electronics and Bharat Earth Movers Ltd. are putting in integrated efforts to speed up the final fabrication stage. This missile programme has been well designed to meet the needs of all the three services. The Prithvi and the Nag for the Army and Akash and Trishul for the Air force. Both the Prithvi and Trishul can be modified or optimised for use by the Navy for surface to surface firing and surface skimming offensive power respectively.

The thrust of this presentation is also to focus

attention to essential factors if not more on defence preparedness.

We must realise that Policy Planning and Strategy on a macro level are more important than additions to weapons, manpower or support systems.

Need for an open approach

It is in this context one must have Perspective Planning over an extended period of anywhere between five to twenty years. In other words our outlook has to undergo radical change as we have been doing in the field of build up of economic infrastructure in our country. We have taken a very bold step, infact a revolutionary one, in striking a balance between public ownership and control to a liberalised economy throwing open vast avenues of business and industry not only to private sector in India but to direct investment from abroad.

Keeping this in mind we have to evolve a policy of an open door approach and access to the defence sector establishments including Ordnance Factories, both in terms of exports, and induction of technology. The present day policy of outmoded secrecy for the sake of secrecy is a fallacy because whenever imports are made from abroad the seller invariably comes to know what we are doing or plan to do.

The mention of this factor has become imperative because of abnormally slow rate of progress by the defence sector undertaking at Bolangir in Orissa for manufacture of critical ammunition for medium and light guns. This project has been bogged down in controversy. This is a classic case of where defence preparedness has suffered due to lack of coherent policy planning.

This is only a tip of the iceberg. Having dragged our feet on a full production line for the T-72M tanks, it has now been decided as a matter of policy to acquire off the shelf these tanks of advanced versions and also secure technology for their production in India. Infact, as a matter of wrong policy the manufacture of T-72 was stalled with unwarranted claims of imminent productionisation of Indian Arjun MBT.

Another example of faltering and vacilating policy is the induction of AJT and advanced combat aircraft for the Indian Air Force. No doubt it is very wise proposition to perservere with the LCA project to achieve self-sufficiency but to peg India's defence on a system that is yet to make its appearance is too much of a gamble. Fortunately, the present government has been prudent enough to seek at least an additional aquardron of MIG-29 fighter aircraft and given its approval for the induction of Sukhois-30 to give the IAF required strength to take care of national security requirements.

The Indian Armed Forces have many outstanding achievements to their credit. However, as war or any external threat requires total mobilisation in a democracy, maximum transparency alone can ensure cooperation on the part of the people in all respects, says the author.

Independent India was born in the midst of hostilities in Jammu and Kashmir. The holocaust that followed the partition of the country, the migration of people and the sudden attack by pakistan in Kashmir valley in October, 1947 created a feeling of insecurity among the people. The armed forces left behind by the Britishers and the infrastructure then available however proved adequate enough to repulse the Pakistani mischief.

Subsequently, the easy manner in which we secured the integration of Junagarh, Hyderabad and Goa brought in an element of overconfidence. Truely speaking, we were lost in an attitude of complacency believing in the good intentions of our neighbours, particularly China.

The rude shock delivered by China in Oct., 1962 made the leaders at the helm of affiars realise the need for an all weather Army, Navy and Air Force. Fear and insecurity hasd then gripped the people and some had even doubted our capability to protect the territorial integrity of the country. People in the North-East, for a moment, felt they were left to fend for themselves. In the background of these developments, one can say that planning for defence preparedness had its beginning after the humiliating Chinese invasion in the North-East.

Thanks to the assistance extended by the then Soviet Union in the development of our Air Force, Navy and Army, besides the help provided by the United Kingdom and France for expansion and modernisation of sea and air elements, we were able to check a renewed Pakistani onslaught in Jammu and Kashmir and Rann of Kutch in Gujarat in 1665. Pakistan was well and truely beaten and the Tashkent Peace Accord held good till 1971.

Gradual build up

Meanwhile, all the three defence services were gradually building up their strength in terms of armour, aircraft carrier, submarines and air defence fighters. Thus when in 1971, after Sheikh Mujibur Rehman gave a call for a mass freedom struggle on March, 26 in Dacca, the Indian armed forces were definitely in a position of superiority to take on the challenge to protect millions of refugees as well as the borders.

During the last 25 years, defence preparedness, as linked to Policy Planning, has been on an ad-hoc basis, if not in fits and starts. No doubt, there has been the acquisition of the T-72M tanks and the BMP series covering the Infantry Combat Vehicle and the Bofors 155 MM field howitzers. The Navy has gained in the acquisition of the Kilo class submarines, the aircraft carrier Viraat and the West German Hunter Killer class submarines.

The Air force has been steadily strengthened with the induction of the Jaguars, MIG-21, MIG-25, MIG-23, 27 and 29. The Mirage 2000, the AN-32 and the IL-76 long haul transports have also added punch to the Air Force. But this by no means reflects a long—term defence policy planning since all these acquisitions virtually came long after the requirements were made known, resulting in heavy cost escalations.

And some of them were clouded in controversies. As a result of which for nearly a despite urgent needs being repeatedly highlighted by the Armed Forces.

Training institutions

Sainik schools

Sainik schools prepare boys academically and physically for entry into National Defence Academy. There are 18 sainik schools in the country, one in each state, except in Nagaland, Meghalaya, Tripura, Sikkim, Arunachal Pradesh, Mizoram and Goa. These schools are affiliated to the Central Board of Secondary Education and follow the 10+2 pattern, in science stream.

Admission is made to class VI on the basis of an all-India entrance examination held every year in February, in which boys in the age group of 10-11 years are eligible to appear. From 1992-93 academic session lateral admission to class IX has also been started for which the boys have to be 13-14 years of age on 1st July of that year. Since its inception, a total of 4,647 boys from these schools were selected for admission to the National Defence Academy, Naval Academy, Armed Forces Medical College etc.

National defence academy

The National Defence Academy (NDA), Khadakwasla, is a Joint Services Training Institution which imparts academic as well as service training. The NDA has been brought in step with the national education format of 10+2+3. The syllabus of the Academy was reviewed to meet these requirements and has been approved by the Jawaharlal Nehru University for the grant of BA/B.Sc degree, at the time of passing out from Academy. the first course commenced training on revised syllabi in January 1989. After passing out from the NDA, the cadets go to their respective service acadmies for further training before being commissioned as officers in the Armed Forces. The present authorised training strength of the Army, Navy and Air Force cadets at the Academy is 1,800. This includes cadets from Bhutan and other friendly countries on as required basis.

Indian military academy

The Indian Military Academy (IMA), Dehra Dun caters for training of cadets for commission into the Army. Cadets join the Indian Military Academy as per the following modes of entry: (a) on passing out from NDA, (b) on graduation from the Army Cadet College which is a wing of the IMA itself, (c) Direct entry graduate cadets who join on qualifying at the Union Public Service Commission Examination and the Services Selection Board, and (d) Technical graduates and University Entry Scheme. The present authorised strength of trainees at the IMA is 1,200 which includes cadets from Bhutan, Shri Lanka, Maldives, Mauritius and Nepal. The authorised training strength of Army Cadet College is 450.

Officers training academy

The Officers Training Academy (OTA), Madras imparts pre-commission training for the following type of courses, (a) Short Service Commission Course of 44 weeks for university graduates who quality in the Union Public Service Commission; (b) course of six months for lady cadets (Women Special Entry Scheme); (c) Permanent Commission on Special List (PC) (SL) to selected service candidates, who qualify after a training of four weeks and (d) Regimental Commission Course for selected service candidates, who qualify after a training of 13 weeks duration. Authorised training strength of the Academy is 500. So far 50 lady cadets have been granted Short Service Commission.

Rashtriya Indian military college

Education on public school lines is imparted at the Rashtriya Indian Military College (RIMC), Dehradun principally for the boys who subsequently desire to join the NDA with a view to obtaining a commission in the Armed Forces. The College runs classes from eighth to 10+2 class. Selection for the RIMC is through a written examination cum *viva voce* conducted through the state governments. Intake into the RIMC is bi-annual.

National defence college

Inaugurated by Pandit Nehru in 1960, the National Defence College is an Inter-Service Organisation functioning under the Ministry of Defence. The NDC is the highest defence institution in India imparting instructions on all elements of national security and strategy to officers due to become Major Generals and equivalent and attain similar status in the Civil Service. The aim is to equip these policy makers with the necessary background and understanding of the total system of economic, political, military, scientific, international relations, national organisational aspects and the planning necessary for national security, both in its internal dynamics as well as the external comulsions. The head of the College is the Commandant, with five faculty members from the Army, Navy, Air Force, IAS, IFS and an administrative staff.

Army cadet college

Army Cadet College is a Wing of IMA which caters for the training of service cadets selected for commission.

The academic format is similar to the NDA on the lines of 10+2+3, and the syllabus is common. On completion of the course these cadets also qualify for a BA/BSc degree recognised by the Jawaharlal Nehra University.

Other training centres and schools

The College of Combat, Mhow conducts the higher command, senior command and junior command courses for Army officers. It also conducts a Combined Operational Review and Evaluation (CORE) programme for selected senior officers of the rank of Major General and equivalent of the three Services once every year. College of Military Engineering, Kirkee (Pune), imparts training to the officers and other ranks in all aspects of military engineering. Long courses of over two years duration are also conducted to train officers up to degree standards. Military College of Telecommunication Engineering, Mhow imparts basic and advanced technical training in telecommunications and signal tactics. Armoured Corps Centre and School, Ahmednagar, conducts training in tactical handling of armoured fighting vehicles, driving and maintenance. School of Artillery, Deolali, provides training in field branch artillery. The Air Defence Guided Missiles School at Gopalpuron-sea trains personnel of the Air Defence Artillery. The High Altitude Warfare School located at Gulmarg and Sonmarg train personnel in the art of mountain warfare including rock, snow and ice-craft. The Counter Insurgency and General Warfare School, Viairengate, trains officers and men in the art of combating insurgency.

Mechanised Infantry Regimental Centre conducts basic and technical training for recruits of mechanised infantry. In addition, it runs basic and instructor courses on anti-tank guided missiles for officers, JCOs and other ranks of mechanised infantry. It also carries out conversion training of units when they are converted to mechanised infantry or when change in equipment is involved. College of Materials Management, Jabalpur, imparts specialised training in materials management including ammunition and explosives and also in contemporary materials management techniques. Some of the other Army training centres and schools are Army Service Corps School, Bareilly; EME School, Vadodara; Military College of Electronics and Mechanical Engineering, Secunderabad; College of Defence Management, Secunderabad; Remount and Veterinary Corps Centre and School, Meerut; Army Eucation Corps Training College and Centre, Pachmari; Army School Physical Training, Pune; Army/Air Transport School, Agra; Military Intelligence Training School and Depot, Pune; Army School of Mechanical Transport, Bangalore; Corps of Military Police Centre and School, Bangalore; Institute of Military Law, Kamptee; Armed Forces Medical College Pune; Institute of National Integration, Pune and Army Medical Corps Centre and School, Lucknow.

National security and conflict resolution

The international milieu

It is possible to construct a scenario from recent events to conclude that the end of history has been reached by the cessation of the Cold War resulting in the disintegration of the Soviet Union/Warsaw Pact and the triumph of liberal democracy over Communism. A palpable reduction of interational tensions has indoubtably occurred at the uppermost hierarchical levels of the international system, with competition shifting into the economic sphere wherein future contentions might arise between the United States, Germany and Japan. Appreciating the resurgence displayed by its economy China seems destined to play a growing political role in North-east and South-east Asia, although some caution would be necessary herein and political conformism would eventually emerge.

There is some controversy, however, whether 'total war' in the Clausewitzian sense has become obsolete since the end of the Cold War, because the support/ assistance of the rival super-powers is no longer available to regional adversaries. Indeed, the efforts of the United States, and the major powers, are more likely to be harnessed for the prevention of conflict, with the United Nations being utilised in more extensive peace keeping roles. Conventional wars, too, have become very destructive with the availability of high technology precision-guided weapons that combine great lethality with high accuracy, as was displayed in Operation "Desert Storms". For these reasons, it could be urged that the possibility of conventional wars, quite apart from nuclear conflict, is steadily becoming remote if not wholly obsolete in future.

But another source of potential contention, if not conflict, arises from North-South issues that are becoming sharply delineated in the spheres of trade and intellectual property rights. These issues, too, would be overshadowed by the technological hegemonism that is being sought by the developed countries over the international system and is embedded in their concerted steps to deny dual-purpose technologies to developing countries on the grounds that they could also be used for military purposes. The control regimes established for purposes of denying/regulating the flow of these technologies–Nuclear Suppliers Groups, Missile Technology Control Regime, Australia Group and COCOM to name the most prominent–have been invigorated and directed to apply their guidelines with greater severity. More disconcertingly, the list of goods, materials, subisidiary items and technologies including within these guidelines for gating are being progressively increased with result that, in a recent case, fertiliser manufacturing technology was denied to India on the tenuous grounds that it could be used for the production of heavy water that could be used in atomic energy reactors which might be used to make fissile materials for nuclear weapons. This situation delineates two possibilities for the evolving technological international order. It could either lead to the establishment of a new colonialism by the developed over the developing world, or it could encourage the developing countries to seek greater cooperation among themselves and work together in the direction of greater self-reliance, if not self-sufficiency. Yet another possibility would be for the technologically more advanced among the countries of the South configuration of nations to enter into mutual arrangements to either generally, or specifically, explore frontier areas of science and technology for cooperative exploitation.

It would be imprudent to suggest that conflict per se, in its numerous manifestations, would become remote and obsolete. The growth of beliefs in the equality of nations in the international system and the spread of the democratic idea and principles of human rights within nations has led to the encouragement of an ethnic consciousness, resulting in movements that seek greater autonomy and even separatism within nation-states. Some weightage no doubt must be given to national/ regional particularities. But the rise of subnationalism in violent forms within the erstwhile Soviet Union and Yogoslavia, for instance, reveals the conflict potential in this new ethnic consciousness, that could affect peace and stability in regional configurations, no less than the nationalism which distinguished the struggles in Vietnam and Afghanistan. It is wholly plausible that external powers might pursue their national interests by intervening such internecine domestic conflicts and exacerbate its dimensions, which presents a generic problem for the international community.

Indeed, the problem of ethno-political consciousness asserting itself highlights the internal roots of conflit coming to the foreground in the international security system during the eighties for causes ranging from the denial of political rights to economic exploitation to identity submergence of ethnic populations within a larger group.

External publicity

Publicity priorities focus largely on image-building and areas of India's unique enduring features such as her luminous history; rich cuvilisation, ethnic, linguistic and cultural variety; diverse and profound religious and philosophical trrraditions; democratic and secular political culture and institutions;pluralistic, tolerant and accommodative social ethos; wide experience in nation-building; and impressive economic and technological achievements. The function of current publicity is to explain and interpret India's foreign policy objectives and actions, and gain acceptance and support for them and intensification of publicity of India's new economic environment and policies. It has been the endeavour of the Ministry of External Affairs to counter unfair and biased reportage by transparency, and to project a balanced perspective through the mainstream media and other opinion-making channels.

To meet the challenge of the world-wide information revolution, the Ministry of External Affairs is gearing up its communications technology by moving to an integrated use of communication by fax and computers as a first step. New publicity and public relations strategies are also being adopted in an effort to keep pace with the changing scenario.

Indian missions abroad arranged telecasts of new documentary fijlms and brought out special supplements in local newspapers on the occasion of Independence Day 1994 and/or arranged telecasts of films to mark the 125th birth anniversary of Mahatma Gandhi.

India's response to negative reports and perceptions on Jammu and Kashmir has been to remind the world about the correct historical background leading to the unambiguous legal accession of Jammu and Kashmir to India, the circumstances leading tot he UN Resolutions on Jammu and Kashmir, the reaffirmation and endorsement of this option by the people and political parties of Jammu and Kashmir through successive elections held under the Indian Constitution and by the Constitutent Assembly, the non-fulfilment by Pakistan of crucial requirements under the Un Resolutions resulting in its non-implementation and absolescence, and the supression of the UN Resolutions with the signing of the Shimpla Agreement enshrining a solemn commitment by India and Pakistan to sort out all problems bilaterally.

Overseas Indians

There are nearly 14 million overseas Indians all over the world who include Indian citizens settled abroad as also persons of Indian origin who have taken foreign citizenship. Government is sensitive to the emotional urges and cultural bonds that overseas Indians have with India as also to their deeply felt desire to nurture their roots in the mother country. Government makes every effort to remain informed about their well-being. Consular work with regard to Indian nationals abroad continued to get constant attention. Indians in Rwanda and Yemen were evacuated to Indian due to internal problems in those countries. Indian Missions in Kampala, Sana'a, Aden and Djibouti rendered assitance to these persons by issuing them duplicate travel documents and arranging for their transportion back to India. Missions abroad provide assistance to Indians insettling differences with local employers, repatriation of destitute Indians, maintaining contacts with Indians in foreign jails, assisting with formalilties for Indians who have died abroad, either in the performance of last rites or return of the dead body to India.

Propagation of Hindi abroad

The Ministry of External Affairs in its endeavour to propagate Hindi abroad extends all possible help to foreign universities, educational institutions and individuals engaged in promotion of Hindi through Indian Missions. During 1994-95, Hindi typewriters/ computers softwards were provided to foreign institutions/individuals. Indian Mission in Buenos Aires, Budapest, Ulaan Baateor, Seoul, Paramaribo, Port of Spain, London and Port Louis contimued to play a major and significant role propagation of Hindi. The High Commission of India, London organised *Kavi Sammelans* in Manchester and London which were attended by poets from India while the Indian Embassy in Kathmandu organised a Hindi-Nepal *Kavi Sammelan*. The Indian Missions in Paramaribo, Budapest and Kathmandu successfully organised *Hindi Diwas* wherein natives of the respective countries participated actively and enthusiastically.The Ministry liaised with Department of Education, *Kendriya Hindi Sansthan,* Agra and Indian Missions abroad for nomination of suitable foreign candidates for scholarship to study Hindi at Kendriya Hindi Sansthan, Agra.

7

India's Foreign Affairs

The kingpin of India's foreign policy has broadly been dictated by a principle of equidistance form the Superpower rivalry until the dissolution of the Soviet Union. In any assessment of India's role to ensure global peace, non-aligned movement played an important part. Although the movement never functioned on any bloc concept, it became the voice of vast multitudes of people spanning four continents belonging to the developing world.

The non-aligned movement was launched in Belgrade in 1961. Eminent statesmen who pioneered the movement were Prime Minister Jawaharlal Nehru, President Tito of Yugoslavia and President Gamel Nasser of Egypt. The movement which had only a handful of members initially later grew into a formidable number. The current chairmanship of Colombia, once believed to be an Americanally in Latin America, is a clear proof that the movement's appeal was spreading to South America, usually considered as "backyard" of US sphere of influence.

The disappearance of the Soviet Union brought an end to Superpower rivalry. It had its effect on the non-aligned movement. Except the coordinating bureau of non-aligned countries at the United Nations, the movement never though it appropriate to have a headquarters. This never gave rise to absence of cohesion in the movement's functioning. In contrast, the Organisation of Africa Unity (OAU) has its headquarters in Addis Ababa, while the Arab League is located in Caero.

Non-aligned movement could have been more powerful as a political force at international level had China preferred to join it. Mao Zedong divided the world into "three worlds" according to the level of economic development. Surely, China fitted in with the concept of "third world", embracing the developing countries. But at no point of time since 1961China a expressed the desire to be part of non-aligned movement, although China rightly belongs to the developing world.

India's third conribution to world peace came from its unremitting support to the anti-apartheid movement in South Africa and its support to decolonisation. New Delhi never gave up the cause of the black South Africans and the Black Africans in the rest of the continent, despite repression on their movement and denial of basic human rights by the colonising powers. One after the other, the French, Portuguese and Dutch colonisers left territories ruled by them. But South Africans were yet to see the light at the end of the tunnel.

The paths to peace and freedom and equal rights were strewn with thorns and hurdles were placed at all steps. the White rule became a blot on the world conscience. Denial to right to live brought an upsurge among the Black South Africans. In their struggle, they found India and the Indians settled there as a great source of inspiration. It was not because Mahatma Gandhi's association with South Africa in the initial years of his political life that made India so receptive to the aspirations of the Black South Africans.

Perhaps in the South African freedom movement and struggle for equality was seen the same psyche of the Indian people who suffered humiliation, imprisonment and torture in India during the long independence struggle. Indians felt genuinely for the Black South Africans. So did the goverment.

In less than a decade's existence as an independent nation, India brought before the world a new concept of governance based on the principle of "Panchsheel". It was but natural for a country that has a long tradition of tolerance. India with numerous languages and multiplicity of religion itself symbolises co-existence. Mutual respect for each other, irrespective of differences, demonstrates Indian ethos.

It is in this context, the Bandung conference in April 1955 that adopted "Panchsheel" created a new concept for the world already handed over to violence and turmoil. The Bandung conference had five proponents: India, Indonesia, Burma, Sri Lanka and Pakistan. The Bandung conference was preceded by the bombing of the Air India plane carrying delegates and journalists over South China sea. Evidently, forces that wanted the settlement of disputes through terrorism asserted their right to show their way of solving issue and problems.

India and the world

India's main foreign policy objectives are based on peaceful co-existence, self-reliance and co-operation, non-alignment, support for de-colonisation, disarmament, restructuring of the inequitous International Economic Order and the global fight against racialism. India's first Prime Minister, Jawaharlal Nehru, laid down the basic parameters of India's foreign policy and his unique contribution was the concept of non-alignment. The fundamental aim was to preserve India's freedom of option and decision-making in an autonomous way, in a world bristling with animosities and block antagonism. Consistent with our traditional values, Nehru ceaselessly promoted the universal cause of disarmament, racial equality, international cooperation for economc develpment and the peaceful resolution of disputes and gave India a conceptual framework which was based on cooperative and peaceful co-existence and non-violence which we continue to adopt in evolving our foreign policy. Basic considerations which governed the structuring of our foreign policy and its implementation are: preservation of India's national identity as a plural democratic and secular society, India's territorial integrity, and well-being of our people. Indian peace-keeping operations formed an element in India's foreign policy, being reflective of India's desire to play a positive role to promote normality at a time of need on the part of certain friently developing countries in difficulties.

India's neighbours

Nepal

Indo-Nepal relations which have been a long tradition of friendship and shared history and culture continued to develop smoothly during 1994-95. Several high-level visits took place between India and Nepal which include the crown prince of Nepal's first official visist abroad to India in August 1994. India-Nepal economic relations also gained from the liberalisation of both economies and from the stable and positive framework provided by the Treaties of Trade and Transit. Nepalese exports to India during 1993-94 were worth Rs. 1,176.3 million and imports from India were worth Rs. 7,874.63 million. The new Sirsiya bridge at the Raxaul border linking the two countries at the point where the traffic in goods and people is the heviest, was completed. The Rajbiraj industrial estate was formally handed over to Nepal.

Bhutan

Economic cooperation between India and Bhutan has provided a solid basis for a close and warm relationship marked by mutual understanding. the King of Bhutan,

Jigme Singye Wangchuk visited India privately in December 1994 when he met the President and the Prime Minister. india is actively involved in implementing portions of Bhutan's Seventh Five Year Plan (1992-97). Major projects such as the airport terminal building at Paro, Kurichu Hydel Project in Eastern Bhutan, hospitals, schools, roads and bridges, transmission lines, rural electrification, survey project, etc., are underway. India also continued to cooperate with Bhutan in the field of higher education, survey and training, and for renovation of culturally important places.

Bangladesh

The level of interaction between India and Bangladesh remained high during 1994-95 by exchange of several high level visits. The first meeting of Indo-Bangladesh Joint Working Group took place in New Delh to discuss, *inter alia,* security-related issues, cross-border movements, the existing visa regime, and the situation along Indo-Bangladesh border. The Border Security Force and the Bangladesh Rifles also held talks in New Delhi and Dhaka to discuss illegal immigration of Bangladesh is into India, trans-border crimes and repatriation of Chakma refugees from Tripura to Bangladesh. During February to August 1994, 5,198 Chakma refugees from Tripura were repatriated to Bangladesh strictly on voluntary basis.

Inspite of India's efforts for arriving at a long-term comprehensive and equitable arrangement on water-sharing, Bangladesh continued to raise the issue in international fora. On 20 December 1994, the Bangladesh Festival of Arts was inaugurated jointly by the Bangladesh Ministry for Cultural Affairs and India's Deputy Ministry of Education and Culture in New Delhi. The second meeting of the Indo-Bangladesh Joint Business Council was held in Dhaka in August 1994. On

4 January 1995, Bangladesh Railway signed a US dollar 10 million agreement with RITES to purchase 10 diesel metre gauge locomotives. India's exports to Bangladesh in 19930-94 were valued at Rs. 1,349.69 crore while imports from Bangladesh were Rs. 56.09 crore.

Myanmar

India's working relationship with Myanmar continued to improve during 1994-95. There were several exchanges of visits between India and Myanmar. During the visit of a Survey delegation from Myanmar to India, operational matters relating to boundary demarcation were discussed. Official level talks with Myanmar for operationalisation of the Border Trade Agreement were held in January 1995. Twenty-eight trainees from Myanmar came to India in 1994-95 for course on farm machinery, computers, news agency operations, journalism, survey, diplomacy, banking, railways and telecommunications. India continued to support the restoration of democratic government in Myanmar.

Sri Lanka

Relations with Sri Lanka continued to be based on friendship, understanding and good neighbourliness. India conveyed her interest in further boosting bilateral ties to Chandrika Bandarnaike Kumaratunga who assumed office as Prime Minister in August 1994. India also expressed her shock at the tragic assasination of UNP Presidential candidate and offered the forensic and ballistic assistance in the investigation of the assasination. The Sri Lankan Foreign Minister visited India in October 1994 and briefed the Indian leadership about the Sri Lanka Government's agenda including the peace process, constitutional reforms and economic policies and stressed Sri Lanka's keenness for sound and cordial relations with India and the Government of India fully reciprocated these sentiments.

The second session of the Indo-Sri Lanka Joint Commission held in New Delhi in April 1994 decided on several measures such as the restoration of preferential tariff margins on Sri Lankan cloves, reduction in tariffs on select items of export interest to Sri Lanka such as ceramic tiles, glycerine, graphite and rubber; extension of a new line of dollar-denominated credit; permission to Bank of Ceylon to open a branch in Madras; and enhanced seat capacity for airlines following civil aviation talks in July 1994. Indo-Sri Lanka trade stood at Rs. 877.3 crore from January to August 1994 with exports valued at Rs. 830.8 crore and imports from Sri Lanka valued at Rs. 46.5 crore. About 8,000 Sri Lankan Tamil refugees returned to their home country in 1994 on a voluntary basis.

Maldives

The traditionally close and friendly relations with Maldives were further strengthned and consolidated during 1994-95. President Maumoon Abdul Gayoom pad a State visit to India in March 1994 and held wide ranging talks with Indian leaders. There were also visits by a parliamentary delegation led by the Speaker of the Citizens' *Majlis,* Maldives Minister of State for National Defence and Security for discussions regarding the operations of Air Maldives to India, which began shortly thereafter, and by Minister of Health and Welfare of Maldives. Ships of the Indian Coast Guard visited Maldives in April 1994 and conducted joint exercises with the ships of Maldivian National Security Service. The Indira Gandhi Memorial Hospital at Male commenced out-patient work on 15 October 1994 where 56 Indian deputationists are stationed to help start work in the hospital. Fifty-nine Maldivian nominees received training in India during 1994-95 in various fields such as medicine, nursing, etc.

Pakistan

India-Pakistan bilateral relations continued to show a downward trend. Pakistan's sustained efforts to internationalise the Kashmir issue, its unabated support to subversion and terrorism directed against India, its intransigence on the issue of resumption of a bilateral dialogue with India, and its persistent negative approach have vitiated the atmosphere and prevented and meaningful progress in bilateral relations. In addition to training, equipping, funding and guiding militants, Pakistan has stepped up its transborder terrorism by inducting mercenaries from third countries into Jammu and Kashmir. India has strongly urged Pakistan to conduct inter-state relations as a responsible member of the international community and to eschew the threat of terrorism held against India. Consistent with her policy to resolve defferences with Pakistan bilaterally and peacefully in accordance with the Shimla Agreenment, India has conveyed to Pakistan on several occasions her readiness for the resumption of bilateral dialogue without any pre-conditions. In March 1994, Foreign Secretary renewed the offer for the resumption of Foreign Secretary-level talks. The Minister of State for External Affairs, Shri R.L. Bhatia reiterated India's offer of dialogue when he met Pak Foreign Minister in July 1994 at Dhaka. Foreign Secretary followed this up with a letter to his Pakistan counterpart inviting him for talks. On 3 November 1994, India once again formally conveyed to Pakistan her offer for dialogue. During his visit to Islamabad in November 1994 to attend the Commonwealth Senior Officials Meeting (COSM), Foreign Secretary conveyed to his Pak counterpart India's readiness to discuss all bilateral issues. The Human Resource Development Minister during his visit to Pakistan to attend the Commonwealth Education Ministers Meeting (November 1994) reiterated India's desire for normalisation of relations. Unfortunately, Pakistan's response has been conditional and negative.

India propose on 7 April and 12 July 1994 to hold consultation for a review of the implementation of the Code of Conduct for treatment of diplomatic/consular personnel in India and Pakistan, in the light of numerous incidents of intimidatory surveillance and harassment meted out to the Indian diplomatic officials and their family members posted in Indian Missions in Pakistan. This proposal, however, did not find favour with Pakistan. Pakistan has persisted with her restrictive visa policy and other negative measures which further impeded people-to-people contacts between the two countries. On 17 March 1994, Pakistan unilaterally and without justification announced the closure of its Consulate in Bombay. Subsequently, on 26 December 1994, Pakistan asked India to close down the Indian Consulate General in Karachi. These actions of Pakistan are regret-table and are patently designed to create perception of tension between the two countries. Pakistan also assumed an exaggerated air of panic towards the isolated reports of incidents of plague in India.

Pakistan's campaign to internationalise and communalise the Kashmir issue continued. At the 50th session of the UNHRC (March 1994), Pakistan had decided to move a resolution on the Human Rights situation in Jammu and Kashmir and aggressively campaigned for support but, subsequently, withdrew its resolution at the behest of a number of friendly countries. At the 49th session of the UNGA, Pakistan made yet another attempt to table a resolution. However, this attempt also failed. In the face of Pakistan's campaign of Jammu and Kashmir issue, India apprised the international community of the politically motivated act by Pakistan and emphasised that all outstanding issues between the two countries need to be resolved peacefully and bilaterally within the framework of the Shimla Agreement.

Afghanistan

There have been some high level exchanges with Afghanistan in 1994 in spite of the unstable conditions in that country. Afghan Minister for Civil Aviation visited New Delhi twice in Macrh and July 1994 as a Special Envoy of Afghan President. Afghan Ministers for Martyrs and Disabled Affairs and for Agriculture paid visits to India in 1994. India has been able to resume some technical cooperation (training facilities, scholarships, medical facilities, etc.) during 1994. India has an abiding concern for welfare and prosperity of the Afghan people. During 1994, India supplied tea, medicines, etc., worth Rs. one crore as relief assistance to Afghanistan. India stands for a united, stable, non-aligned and independent Afghanistan, and supports a peaceful political settlement which is acceptable to all sections of the people of Afghanistan and the ongoing peace initiative of the UN, and stands ready to make a contribution to peace efforts.

India and the world

In 1972 Prime Minister Indira Gandhi emphasized at the UN Conference on Human Environment at Stockholm that the removal of poverty is an integral part of the goal of an environmental strategy for the world. The concepts of interrelatedness, of a shared planet, of global citizenship, and of 'spaceship earth' cannot be restricted to environmental issues alone. They apply equally to the shared and interlinked responsibilities of environment and development. The global community must address the issue of global development in order to move towards and environmentally sound planet.

But the problem of poverty remains as serious today as it was then. Speaking recently at the opening meeting of UNCTAD at Colombia, UN Secretary-General Boutros Boutros Ghali emphasized poverty as one of the most urgent issues facing the international community. It is the goal of removing poverty, of development at the global level, which must be addressed if environmental problems are to be tackled.

The South has a difficult task ahead of it. It has to achieve economic development with minimum damage to its environment, for this alone can sustain development. Unlike colonial powers that could exploit the vast resources of their colonies and industrialize rapidly, and pollute the global ecosystem, the developing countries today are searching for more sustainable and environment friendly solutions. But these solutions have a cost. The developing countries would require access to the latest technologies that would enable them to avoid the dirty-industry route to development.

History has led to vast inequalities, leaving almost three—fourths of the world's people living in less developed countries and one-fifth below the poverty line. The long—term impact of past industrialization, exploitation and environmental damage cannot be wished away. It is only right that development in the remaining part of this century and in the next be more conscious of its long—term impact. Our common future can only be achieved with a better understanding of our shared responsibility. Shared responsibility for the present and the past.

At a global level, the common future depends on sustaibable use of natural resources. The current pattern of development based on high resource consumption, high waste and low recycling, as practised in the North, is not sustainable and yet it is in this direction that much of the South is heading.

The alternative paradigm of improving standards of living without infliciting heavy environmental damage poses its own problems. Many of the technologies required are new, some are as yet being developed. the major costs of pollution control, and the limiting options from an environmental point of view, are factors that the early developing countries in the North did not have to consider. However, it is the cost of these more stringent norms that is the price of development today. These costs need to be shared if the developing countries of the South are to follow an alternative path. A path that bypas the route of severe environmental damage.

Sharing responsibility means sharing costs, rather than charity or aid. Funding mechanisms that are essentially donor driven need to be replaced by moe open participatory mechanisms which involve developed and developing nations. It si inherent in the concept of shared responsibility that funding becomes obligatory, rather than an optional charity. It is only on this basis that we can approah the building of a common future.

Developing countries are equal partners in any process that discusses global issues like environment and development. Their inputs are essential in decision—making to bring in local perspectives and to prevent generalized solutions. Evolving alternatives can only be done through a proper understanding of the local situation. This is best done where decision-making is not centralized.

Environmental standards and mechanisms to deal with environmental issues also need to be worked out on a country by country basis, if not in a more decentralized way. An international funding mechanism or a trade policy should not become the insturment to impose environmental conditionalities.

The countries of the south are among the richest in terms of biodiversity. This biodiversity is the source of a number of products that today benefit all humankind. Advances in biotechnology have increased the range of products in pharmaceuticals, agriculture etc. by modifying and combining the genetic resources collected largely from the South. With the much greater financial and research capability in the North, these new products are being made available through companies of the developed world. When the original genetic resources was collected there was no payment made to the country from which it came. Today these living resources are being patented and sold aback, often to the very countries from which the original genes may have been taken.

Issues of biodiversity must be discussed along with the sharing of biotechnology, sharing of the results of R & D and the commercial benefits derived from the bio-materials. The traditional knowledge base of the rural and indigenous communitites is usually the starting point for identifying particular species for particular applications. This must be kept in mind in any discussion of intellectual property rights (IPR) related to biotechnology. Indigenous communities have over centuries worked towards developing and improving crop varieties. For instance the more than 50,000 varieties of rice found in India have provided a tremendous base for research on rice. One recognizes that biotechnology research must be adequately compensated. But mechanisms other than the presently prevalent system of intellectual property rights are required. The researcher has to be compensated without restricting use as implied in IPR.

Access to environment friendly technologies also needs to be easier and much more widespread. In many cases, existing technologies would need to be replaced.

The cost of the new technologies and of pollution control mechanisms is likely to be higher than that of the older processes. However it is important that the wrong decision is not taken owing to short—term financial constraints faced by developing countries. Mechanisms would therefore have to be found to subsidize this change over.

India shares the concern about ozone depletion and understands the need for coordinated action in this area. But it also recognizes that the problem has essentially been created by the developed countries who must also accept the principal responsibility for it. A situation cannot be accepted which while reducing emission levels of CFCs in the North, prohibits even the small levels of CFC-use that arise from refrigeration and other requirements which are, if anything, more necessary in the much hotter tropical countries of the South. The solution is in terms of a quicker and less costly method of transferring the newly developing alternative technologies to the South with international funding mechanisms bearing part of the costs.

India has expressed these concerns in relation to the Montreal Protocol, and now amendments have been made to enable countries such as India to sing it. Of course it must be realized that even today India's CFC consumption is far below levels presecribed by the Protocol. But India has constituted a task froce to draft its own strategy for containing CFC consumption within the country.

Global warming is another concern that India shares with the international community. The scientific basis for calculating some of the figures related to this issue are being debated at the international level and India is bringing its perspective into this discussion. But apart from the details, India is of the view that developed countries, whose total emissions are far larger than those of the South, must shoulder the principal burden of bringing down emissions so that there is a uniform, sustainable per capita emission level. It is inevitable that in this process, countries which are developing will invariably have an increase in emission levels of greenhouse gases arising out of the development process.

In the final analysis, as Mr. Kamal Nath, India's Minister for Environment and Forests, said at the special session of the UNEP Governing Council at Nairobi in February 1992, "It is not a question of assistance or aid, but of global partnership in working towards making our planet healthier, safer and more productive."

International cooperation

India realizes the vital need for international cooperation, bilateral and multilateral programmes and regional initiatives in dealing with issues of environment and development. At the governmental level, the Ministry of Environment and Forests acts as a nodal agency for relations with international agencies like UNEP, SACEP, IUCN, World Bank, FAO, UNDP, SAARC and EEC, Independently, NGOs in India have taken several initiatives towards global cooperation and exchanges of ideas. They have, through dealing with international NGOs and participation in international forums, created awareness of a South perspective. They have played an important part in highlighting some inherent shortcomings in international thinking and in international conventions.

Ozone layer

India acceded to the Vienna Convention for the Protection of the Ozone Layer (March 1985). Under this framework Convention, the Montreal Protocol on Substances that Deplete the Ozone Layer was adopted in

September 1987. This Protocol lays down a timetable for the phasing out of the more widely used CFCs. The Protocol came into force on 1 January 1989. India refused to sign it because of the regional treatment given to developing countries and the large economic burden which would have to be borne by them even though they have contributed almost nothing to the problem. In June 1990 the parties tot he Protocl agreed to comprehensive amendments so that developing countries such as India could participate in the global action without deterimental effects to their economies. India would be able to accede to the Protocol once the London amendments came into force. In any case, India is at present far below the targets specified by the Montreal Protocol.

Migratory species

India signed the Convention on the Conservation of Migratory Species of Wild Animals (the Bonn Convention) in 1979. The convention came into force on 1 November 1983. The Convention on Protection of Migratory Birds between India and the former USSR was retified by both countries and came into force in 1986.

International support

India has received financial and technical support for environment related projects from multilateral institutions like the World Bank, FAO, UNDP, UNIDO and EEC. On a bilateral basis, USA, UK, Japan, Canada, Sweden, Germany, the Netherlands, France, Norway, Australia, and some other countries have been collaborating extensively with India.

Pollution

India is signatory to the International Convention for the Prevention of Pollution of the sea by Oil, 1954 (LOndon); the international convention on Civil Liability for Oil

Pollution Damage (as amended), 1969 (Brussels); the International Covention on the Establishment of an International Fund for Compensation for Oil Pollution Damage (as amended), 1971 (Brussels); the Protocol of 1978 relating to the International Convention for the Prevention of Pollution from Ships; the United Nations Convention on the Law of the Sea, 1982 (Montege Bay); and the Basel Convention on the Control of Transboundary Movements of Hazardous Wastes and their Disposal.

Antarctica

India holds consultative status to the Anatractic Treaty (1959) and is a signatory to the Convention of the Antarctic. India is also considering ratification of a Protocol on Environmental Protection to Antartica under the Antarctica Treaty.

South perspective for UNCED

To further India's efforts toward South cooperation and to evolve a common strategy among the developing countries to deal with global environmental issues, and international conference of 21 developing countries was hosted by India in New Delhi in April 1990. As a follow-up to this, a ministerial level Conference of Developing Countries was organized by the People's Republic of China in Beijing in June 1991, which was the first such conference of developing countries. At this conference, the 41 participating countires adopted a declaration which articulates the concerns of these countries. India participated actively in putting forward the concerns of the Group of 77 countries.

India and world peace

Right from the beginning as a free nation India has chosen the path of non-alignment to ensure global peace. India gave the world a new concept of governance based on the principle of "Panchasheel" and also played a major role as a peacekeeper under the aegis of the United Nations.

In the formulation of foreign policy of any nation, the determining principle is its long-term goal. A large degree of flexibility and predictability is its final reliance and resource.

India's foreign policy, in this broad perspective, has been guided by its commitment to world peace. It is little wonder that India should choose the path of non-alignment right from the beginning as a free nation since 1947.

While assessing India's contribution to world peace over the past half a century, I have chosen to concentrate on the principal pillars on which rest the edifice of foreign policy that has stood the scrutiny of the Indian people. Indian domestic policy has been subject of intense debate by diverse political entities but the foreign policy has almost enjoyed a monopoly of public opinion based on the principle of consensus.

In the order of importance, Indian policy on nuclear-free world and elimination of nuclear weapons aimed at achieving a comprehensive disarmament within a time-frame has been widely acclaimed all the world over.

It is an unequal world in which we live, and also a world in which political expendiency is placed above morality. The 15th century born Italian statesman and political philosopher Machiavelli may have died his physical death in 1527. But his spirit lives on and his doctrine of statecraft indealing with foreign relations still is a guidding star for many nations.

The latest battle that India fought was on the issue of Comprehensive Test Ban Treaty (CTBT) at Geneva and New York. Almost single-handed India put up a lone fight against virtually the rest of the world with the exception of a few likeminded countries. It looked like an instance of being stonewalled by representatives of countries led by nuclear-haves both at the United Nations and at the Conference on Disarmament in Geneva.

Even when it was known that India under no circumstances would agree to the CTBT draft, rest of the delegates representing their respective countries listened to India's point of view with bated breath. Till the last moment India stubbornly stuck to its policy decision that there was no in-between position on total nuclear disarmament.

Critics of India accused it of being inflexible, and the main charge against New Delhi was that it lacked realism in asking for disarmament under a time bound programme. Instead, experts argued that a time-frame of 10 years was realistic. Between now and the end of cold war with the collapse of the Soviet Union in 1991, the global nuclear arsenal has come down to half. Interestingly, the former Soviet President Mikhail Gorbachev's last call for total elimination of nuclear weapons had also set a time limit for 10 to 12 years. In the early nineties nuclear warheads were put at 57,000. This means that more than 28,000 nuclear weapons are still in the possession of nuclear weapon states.

While advocating a step-by-step approach to eliminate nuclear weapons, none of the states possessing them has ever wished to take the first step and make any firm commitment for their elimination.

Among the five permanent Security Council members, China is the only Asian nuclear weapon state. In his analysis of India and the CTBT, Director of Institute for Defence Studies Analyses Jasjit Singh said in the Institute's September 1996 issue, "there are major uncertainties about the future strategic scenario (in Sino-Indian relations)."

Jasjit Singh says: "it needs to be recalled that China carried out a nuclear test within hours of giving a commitment (during the NPT extension conference in 1995) that required the utmost restraint in carrying out nuclear explosions. It has continued to test since then at sites less than 1,000 kilometres from India. According to reports, the US Defence Secretary stated that China has been providing nuclear weapon technlogy to Pakistan in the recent past."

The world knows that India's concern about nuclear proliferation relates to China possessing a nuclear arsenal. That China's sole objective was to become a nuclear weapon state is evident from the fact that China neglected the peaceful use of neclear energy until late eighties. Ten years after China had experimented with its first successful nuclear test in 1964, India entered the nuclear scene for the first time in 1974 and there it has ended,. Besides, Pakistan has a clandestine nuclear programme fully assisted by Chinese technology. For the first time, China publicly asserted that India must ratify the CTBT. A conclusion is inescapable that those who wanted India to ratify the CTBT would have liked to see that India's security interests are mortgaged to other countries.

Indian and South Asian region

As the set of Asian economies achieving impressive economic performance has expanded from the Gang of Four (Korea, Taiwan, Singapore and Hong Kong) to many more (e.g., Thailand, Malaysia, Indonasia and that largest of them all, China), the South Asian region is more of an exception in not participating in this economic transformation in the continent. As the economies to India, Pakistan, Bangladesh, Nepal and Sri

Lanka adjust to the requirements of the newly emerging global economic scenario and restructure their economies of face the new challenges, is there any scope for co-operation and co-ordination? The answer is unambiguously yes. The South Asian Association for Regional Cooperation (SAARC) was born of such perception in December, 1985.

Whatever the achievements and weaknesses of SAARC there is not denying that this regional organisation has created an overall atmoshphere in which it is possible to communicate on regional perspective as viewed from each nation's vantage point. Placed below are a few important economic issues which should be on the agenda for co-operation among the nations present at this conference.

Areas for cooperation

Promoting trade and investment between the countries of the South Asian region is a venture which will benefit them all in course of time. Intra-regional trade is not only less than 3 per cent of the total foreign trade of these countries at present but the share has declined in the eighties. India has large trade surpluses with individual countries in the region. There are pressures from neighbouring countries on India to throw its markets open. While India is passing through a phase of lowering its foreign trade barriers as part of the ongoing process of globalisation, promotion of trade with the SAARC countries is better pursued within the framework Sapta agreement such as (South Asian Preferential Trade Agreement). A framework agreement of SAPTA was signed by SAARC countries and adopted in April, 1993, and concessions by individual countries are to be worked out by December, 1993. Progress on this front, however, has been slow, and Pakistan in particuar has been very slow in the follow up.

An active exploration of trade possibilities and choices within the region does not preclude the option of globalising the individual economies to gain access to investment, technology and markets. Working within a regional framework creates an atmosphere in which some bilateral irritants (e.g., Pakistan's refusal to grant Most Favoured Nation Treatment to India) are easier resolved. Growing economic inter-dependence among countries of the region is also in the long run interest of peace in the region.

The importance of regional infrastructure utilising the enormous potential provided by the resources of the region cannot be emphasised enough. The possibilities and potential in the area of water resources has been extensively analysed in numerous studies at the Centre for Poicy Research. The most recent study concludes that the differences that divide the nations which share the Ganga-Brahamputra-Meghna basin and the quantitative values involved in their water disputes are relatively small compared to the far greater benefit that each of them could realise through co-operation. It recommends that numerous trade-offs can be considered in order to even out specific gains and losses so that South Asia will emerge a stronger region.

In the critical area of food security, steps have already been taken to build a SAARC Food Security Reserve which came into force on August 12, 1988. The Reserve consists of 241,580 tonnes of foodgrains of which India's contribution has been 63 per cent. While the Reserve has not been utilised so far, it holds out the promise of crucial assistance in critical times of need.

As for the common goal of poverty alleviation from the region, there is need for exchanging information and experience in direct programmes for poverty alleviation. The Report of the Independent South Asian Commission on Poverty Alleviation (1992) which was discussed at the 7th SAARC summit in April, 1993, is a good beginning. It was agreed at the summit that a national level pro-poor plan would be drawn up by each member state and the experience and progress will be compared at the next SAARC summit. Co-operation and concerted effort to fight poverty in the region must remain the top priority for the countries of the region.

Guidelines for building a new order in South Asia

Objective conditions are emanating from international change for building a conflict-free cooperative South Asia. Subjective inputs are still lacking, but those who have the destinies of one-sixth of humankind in their hand are coming under increasing pressure from the objective realities that are pathways to a new world order.

The world's growth area has shifted from Europe to the Asia-Pacific. The EEC has shown the way how nations, despite their resistance to parting with national sovereignty, are laying the foundations of economic and technological supranationalism, leading, sooner rather than later, to the foundation of willingly diminished political sovereignty. The Asia-Pacific region is much more diverse and larger than Western Europe. It is a region mostly of newly independent states who carry on their bodies the scars from their struggles for national revolution. In this region, too, several cooperative groupings are either in the process of forming or are conceptually in the air. President Clinton talks of a new Pacific Community and has plans to convene an informal summit next year of the members of the Asia-Pacific Economic Community, which is still to be formally launched. Japan's diplomacy is now vigorously seeking an area of "PARTNERSHIP" with ASEAN and other Asia-Forum with which several non-ASEAN countries like the Indo-China states, China, Japan, the US and even Russia are linked. It is committed to the creation of an ASEAN common market. Gorbachev's cry for an Asia-Pacific Helsinki is now echoed faintly by Bill Clinton and loudly by President Nazarbayev of Kazhakstan. The US, Japan and Korea, together with Taiwan and Hong Kong, are thinking in terms of setting up an East Asian caucus. In the Western hemisphere the U.S. Canada and Mexico have signed an agreement to establish a North American Common Market. Nations of Latin America are in the process of engineering two or perhaps three regional grouping. To be sure, none of these groupings, whether formed or in the process of forming, are from those who have had the old order in their grip for several decades.

South Asia, home of one fifth of human kind, is still lagging behind other regions in coming together for faster economic development and common security. However, SAARC is now committed to create the region as a preferential trade bloc by 1997. Not al SAARC members are equally ethusiastic about the idea, but the fact that none has rejected it is evidence enough to forecast that this conflicted region too cannot live in conflict and in isolation from one another for a long time. The convergences that we see around South Asia cannot skip over our region. In the medium run, Indians and Pakistanis will become good, if not friendly neighbours. Regional cooperation in peace, development and security is now on the agenda of each nation of South Asia and of the region as a whole. As and when the South Asians build their own regional system of economic and security cooperation, they will have to learn from the history of conflicts and from their own indigenous civilsations and heritages. They will need to renounce the use or even the threat of use of force to settle disputes and differences. They will have to resolve their territorial disputes through negotiations. They will not interfere in one another's internal affairs nor allow their respective territories to be used against the inerest of other members of the regional community. Bilateral and regional treaties of cooperative security will guarantee their individual and collective territorial unity, integrity and soveregnty. This will make it possible for them to do with the minimum essential defence expenditures and harvest a peace dividend that will be used to improve people's, conditions of living.

Mass poverty is a cause for insecurity of regimes and states, and South Asia has the dubious distinction of being the home of the world's largest mass of poor and deprived humanity. The countries of South Asia must rebuild their own domestic orders with creation of wealth. From a preferential trade area in theory as well as practice, they have to graduate to a South Asian common market. They will have to create a South Asian pool of technologies and share the benefits of imported high technology. They must learn that improvement in living conditions in any one of the countries countributes to the advancement of the region as a whole. Freindly competition must be the other side of the coin of friendly cooperation.

In a new South Asian order, no nation must aspire after hegemony or sphere of influence. Each one will be the equal of the others. In building relationships with extra-regional powers, each member of the South Asian community will ensure that the interests of no other members are hurt. The weak in the community must receive the constant attention of the strong in the filed of economy and technology. To the extent possible, the community must coordinate and harmonise their increasing international trade. To the maximum degree possible, they must trade directly with one another. Customs barriers will be gradually lifted. South Asians must be able to travel freely with dignity and honour throughout the region, and build regional tourist facilities so that the region a whole becomes a major international tourist attraction. Differences will always arise between and among nations. Cooperation, practised for long years, will minimise differences, as it has happened in ASEAN.

Finally, South Asia will have to fall in line with regional and global trends. One of the most important trends is that institutions, practices and outlooks are becoming more alike across national frontiers. Economic and technological convergences are pressing for national political and defence convergences. Governments are being judged not by their claims to ideological enthusiasm or rectitude, but by their performance. Performance is now determined by answers to a set of questions. Are governments practising or inhibiting development? Are they ensuring a fair distribution of the benefits of development to the weak and are they protecting those who need social protection? Are they improving the quality of life of ordinary people and protecting the environment for their children? Are they conducting foreign policies in ways that reinforce the security and national pride of their regional collectivities. Are the governments being run for the benefit of the governed?

Draft declaration

South Asia must leave behind its legacy of confrontations and conflicts and import from the world and retrieve from its own ancient heritage and culture qualities of cooperative peace, development and security, its leaders and peoples must take up in earnest the long-delayed task of resolving bilateral differences and disputes, and impart to SAARC the synergy of creative regionalism. All countries of South Asia are now democracies. It is imperative therefore of each nation and of the region as a whole to improve the quality of life of its teeming poor and deprived humanity. More than one-half of the billion-plus population in the region lives in abject conditions. South Asia has lived for almost fifty years obsessed with its historical cleavages. Now, as the planet moved towards the third millennium, South Asia must look to the future and build itself as a peer of other regions, which have joined the efforts of likeminded nation-states in collective endeavours to improve the quality of life of the governed.

South Asia is unaware of the rich natural and human resources of the seven nations that constitute the regional community. Now, in the post cold war world, the region is baffled and bewildered by the complexities of its humanscape. Its governments are strained by confrontations and conflicts at the bilateral level, weakened by the failure of the member states to build bridges of cooperation, and afflicted by domestic ethnic and religious cleavages that take a heavy toll of human life. While several other regions of the world have made impressive progress in regional cooperation for development and security, South Asia, home of ancient civilisations and great religions, lags behind them in making the best use of economic and technological convergences that are the hallmark of the era initiated by the end of the cold war.

Insurgencies, ethnic conflicts, caste clashes, sectarian violence, drug traffic, custodial deaths, violation of human rights, and religious fanaticism conspire together to keep South Asia in the backwoods of the modern world. Behind these effusions and fusillades of blood and hatred, however, lies an uprecedented awakening of the long-inert poor and deprived in a region whose societies are mutli-lingual, multi-ethnic, multi-cultural and multi-religious. A South Asia governed on the high principles of social justice and human resource development, will also be a South Asia of good neighbourliness and regional cooperation.

Leadership failures over a long period of time has created a broad divide between People and Power. Entrenched power structures resist participatory democracy with the principle of self-government extended to the frontier village. These interests, sometime linked with external forces, have places a high premium on conflicts and cleavages between South Asian countries. Power structures are often uninterested in horizontal developmeni and unwilling to part with the enormous power and privilege they have enjoyed since independence.

It is the imperative of the presenet and future generations of South Asian peoples to work for a region that will match ASEAN and other regional communities in cooperative development and security. South Asian leaders must without further loos of time address themselves earnestly to conflict management, control and resolution, peaceful solution of divisive issues, the formation, stage by stage, of a common market and a free trade area, giving protection at the same time to weaker industries, and establishing a regional pool of technologies. South Asians must be able to resolve their differences without the intervention of outside powers. Peace is always an offspring of give-and-take, live-and-let-live, of compromises with dignity. Absolutist positions do not make peace.

Above all, South Asians must develop an elevating vision of the future. Their visions must be hewn from the constructive, integrative and cooperative trends and processes released by the collapse of the Berlin Walls of the cold war, not from the rhetoric of threats, and conflicts that still proliferate in the planet. Only united and together can South Asia, in cooperation with other regional organisations in the developing world, sucessfully frustrate efforts by the developed to keep the developing majority of the international community at a level of technological and economic inferiority.

All national constitutions have something akin to a bill of rights, howsoever named. Derogations are permitted but the frequency and facility with which these have been resorted to calls for introspection and review. South Asian nations should be urged to subscribe to various international covenants and instruments and, having done so, must ratify them expenditously. National laws should be reviewed and, where necessary, upgraded to measure up to these international commitments.

The right to development and poverty alleviation is imperative. South Asia must cooperate to improve the quality of life of its people. But all rights are indivisible and there is no hierarchy of rights.

It would be useful to establish links between official and NGO human rights organisations in the region. SAARC could consider an initiative in this regard by establishing a small human rights cell. Strengthening and closer monitoring of the criminal justice system in countries of the region would go far towards underpinning human rights. Special courts could be one remedy. These could promote specialisation and avoid undue delay. Cross-border violations, drug traffiking and migration pose common problems and common danger. Mutual discussion and special mechanisms might be considered to concert action and defuse tensions.

Awareness and legal aid are prime factors in promoting human rights and environmental protection.

Primary education and health and population control are of fundamental importance for the region.

They merit the highest priority in national planning, investments and implementation.

South Asia should develop a common approach to the protection and advancement of its tribal populations who should be encouraged to develop in accordance with their own genius without being treated as separate groups divorced from the mainstream of national life and aspirations of which they are an integral and equal part.

South Asia is made up of plural societies embracing a rich diversity. This plurality, including all minorities, must enjoy equal rights and opportunities.

South Asian societies are deeply religious. There must be respect for all faiths, cultures and traditions. Fundamentalism of whatever brand, poses a threat to harmony and stability in each country and must be constructively countered through education and dialogue.

The environment is a trust. The countries of the region must work to pursue and accelerate policies that will stem degradation and start a restorative process. All new programmes, equipment and infra-structure should be based on upgraded environmental norms. All must strive to conserve nature, promote sustainability, avoid waste and ostentatious consumerism, and ensure greater equity.

While South Asia's environmental concerns are linked to subsistence and survival, it must be willing to cooperate to ameliorate global environmental problems. SAARC should endeavour to evolve a common aproach towards dealing with these global issues and environmental protocols under discussion.

The foregoing discussion would re-emphasise our contention at the beginning of this paper that the choices available to South Asia are plainly evident. It could either proceed to deepen its ties in various spheres of their bilateral relations, especially lower key areas like cultural, economic, social and academic activities to erode the edges of suspicion and mistrust that afflict political relations between the South Asian countries. It would be tragic if, on the other hand, mutual differences continue to exist, and bedevil the relationships between the sub-continental neighbours, and they persist in wasting their resources on activities that have no useful result.

Above all, it requires greater understanding that the locus of tensions and instabilities has shifted from the external to internal polity, and the roots of the problems of internal security, whether they arise from ethnic, communal or socio-economic causes, lie in the absence of a just order. The various forms of deprivation, that include the denial of political, economic or social rights, need to be more seriously addressed by the countries of South Asia in the interests of managing their internal polities in the years to come. For this purpose also, it is very necessary that the tensions and instabilities that confront their external polities from within the region are sought to be resolved by patient and earnest endeavours.

The South Asian association for regional cooperation

The 14th session of the SAARC Council of Ministers held in Dhaka in July 1994 reviewed the progress in the implementation of the Agreement on SAARC Preferential Trading Arrangement (SAPTA). A report adopted by the SAARC Workshop held in New Delhi in March-April representing a collective position was presented at the World Conference on Natural Disaster Reduction held in Yakohama, Japan in May 1994. The Meeting of Finance/ Planning Ministers of SAARC countries held in Dhaka in July 1994 decided that a mechanism should be set up for exchange of information on experiences of the SAARC countries in the implementation of poverty alleviation programmes. The SAARC Ministerial Conference on Youth held in Male in May 1994 adopted a resolution known as "Male Resolution on Youth". SAARC Documentation Centre (SDC) has been established and located at the Indian Scientific and Documentation Centre, New Delhi. India organised a SAARC Meeting of Experts on Rehabilitation Techniques for Disabled Persons from November-December 1994 at the National Institute for Mentally Handicapped, Secunderabad.

South-East Asia and the Pacific

In keeping with India's desire for greater integration with the Asia Pacific, South-East Asia continued to be an area of prime focus during 1994-95. Numerous high-level contacts helped to rekindle interest in India in those countries. Efforts to synergise the complementarity in the economies of India and the region succeeded in numerous productive ventures in both sides. There are 96 joint ventures in countries in South-East Asia. Currently, India's exports to the region are in the range of Rs. 5,500 crore, a little less than 10 per cent of her global exports.

India's bilateral relations with Singapore continued on a dynamic course. Prime Minister's visit to Singapore in September 1994 was instrumental in turning a new chapter in India's relations with Singapore. Public housing, power generation, telocommunications, tourism and civil aviation were identified as sectors for possible cooperation with Singapore in India. The Prime Minister suggested Singapore's involvement in commercialising new technologies developed by CSIR and also flagged India's interest in further strenthening defence cooperation in areas such as training and equipment. a Memorandum of Understanding on Foreign Office Consultations and a dozen corporate agreements were signed during the visit. Prime Minister Goh Chok Tong's visit to India again in January 1995 after his earlier visit in January 1994 signified the growing informality and closeness in the relationship of mutual benefit.

Prime Minister's visit to Vietnam in September 1994 reaffirmed India's traditionally warm and close relationship in the changing environment. While acknowledging the strength and continuity of bilateral relations between India and Vietnam, both sides agreed that there was need to upgrade economic linkages. Several new areas including sugarcane cultivation and processing, dairy farming, rubber plantation and manufacture, vegetable oil production, leather processing, etc., were identified. Four agreements were signed during the visit on Avoidance of Double Taxation, Facilitation of Visas, Defence Cooperation and Foreign Office Consultations. The visiting Indian business delegation also signed six corporate agreements relating to investments and joint ventures in Vietnam.

With Thialand, there is an excellent understanding at the political level reinforced by periodic exchange of high level visits which include the visit of the Thai Parliamentary Committee of Religion, Art and Culture in September 1994, Thai Deputy Foreign Minister's visit in October 1994 and Deputy Prime Minister of Thailand's visit to Calcutta in January 1995 in connection with Confederation of Indian Industries (CII) Centenary celebrations. Secretary-level talks between India and Thailand were also held in January 1995 in New Delhi. The first meeting of the India-Thailand Joint Business Council aslo took place. India's bilateral trade with Thailand showed a welcome sign of growth with the overall value reaching US dollar 601.60 million during 1993-94. From Thialand, investment proposals worth US dollar 120 million (approximately Rs. 360 crore) were approved in 1993. The Aditya Birla group is the largest Indian investor with three joint ventures.

India's close relations with Indonesia continued to be strengthened during 1994-95. The visit, of President Soeharto to New Delhi for the reconvened G-15 Summit in March 1994 offered a fresh opportunity for bilateral exchanges and interaction in diverse fields. The volume of trade in 1993-94 was US dollar 354.36 million against the previous year's figure of US dollar 197.19 million. India has 15 joint ventures in Indonesia with investments worth US dollar 189 million.

Prime Minister Mahathir's special gesture of visiting India in March 1994 for the reconvened G-15 Summit after his visit in the same connection three months earlier, contributed to the strengthening of India's bilateral relations with Malaysia. Several major projects involving Indian companies have been cleared over the last year. There are 18 Indian joint ventures in Malaysia and another 14 under various stages of implementation. Malaysian investment in India continued to look up with approved investment reaching Rs. 830 million in 10 projects in various areas. Over 100 Malaysian Air Force personnel are currently undergoing training in India as per the defence cooperation between both the countries.

With the Philippines, India's relations have remained cordial and friendly. The Foreign Office Consultations in Manila in November 1994 underlined the need to step up bilateral economic cooperation and a Joint Business Council was set up. Meat exports from India to the Philippines resumed after a gap of almost thirty years. Senator Leticia Shahani, President Pro-tempore of the Phillippines Senate visited India twice during 1994-95.

India's relations with Brunei Darussalam are also gathering momentum. Brunei's Minister of Communications visited India in January 1995 when a Memorandum of Understanding was signed to discuss matters relatingto the conclusion of an Air Services Agreement and introduction of scheduled air services between the two countres.

With Camboida, India continues to enjoy close and cordial relations. Former Deputy Prime Minister and Foreign Minister visited India in June 1994. A Memorandum of Understanding on Foreign Office Consultations was signed. It was also decided to establish a centre for artificial limbs in Cambodia.

The Lao Foreign Minister visited India in August 1994 and a Memorandum of Understanding on Technical Cooperation and a Cultural Agreement were signed. The visit imparted a much-needed impetus to the bilateral relations.

Relations between India and Australia continued to be cordial. Vice President Shri K.R. Narayanan visited Australia in April 1994 where he inaugurated the Festival "India Today 1994" a two-month long diversified programme of events featuring arts, music, culture-organised by the Austrialia-India Council. Former Deputy Premier of Victoria visited India in February 1994 to identify specific areas for expanding trade an investment and the Australian Chief of Defence Forces visited in April 1994 besides several business/trade delegations also visited India. The third meeting of the India-Australia Joint Ministerial Commission was held in February 1994 in Sydney. A business cum investment seminar was organised in Sydney and the India-Australian Joint Business Council's meeting held in Perth in April 1994. The bilateral trade during 1993-94 was worth Rs. 2,855.08 crore with adverse balance of trade against India. Australian investment in India has been rising steadily and during January-September 1994 it was Rs. 385 crore, the fourth largest after USA, Germany and

NRIs. An Honorary Consul General of India was appointed in Melbourne in November 1994.

The traditional friendly relations between India and New Zealand were maintained. Bilateral consultations at Secretary-level were held in April 1994 in Wellington. Bilateral trade registered an increase of 20 per cent in 1993-94 to Rs. 342 crore. About 12 joint ventures in various fields have been launched. The fourth meeting of the Indo-New Zealand Joint Business Council was held in Auckland in April 1994 while the fourth meeting of the India-New Zealand Joint Trade Committee was held in Wellington in June 1994.

India has declared that the Fijian Government should accelerate the review process of the racialy-biased 1990 constitution with a view to achieving an early solution acceptable to all the sections of the Fijian population and India has decided to establish diplomatic and consular relations with Federated States of Micronesia, a UN member.

Other Sources of inter-state conflict

If some prominence has been given here to Indo-Pak tensions it is because they constitute the overarching reason for SAARC not developing faster to knit together a pattern of regional cooperation in the region.

Apart from the Indo-Pak contention, in its various dimensions, the other sources of tensions in South Asia that could escalate to inter-State conflict might be recognised to arise from:

(i) Territorial disputes arising from divergent claims over areas in the region;

(ii) Ethnic tensions within nations that spill over inter-State boundaries; and

(iii) Population flows within the region reflecting inter-

State tensions and leading to refugee exodus, or voluntary emigration in search of socio-economic betterment.

Territorial disputes are, prominently, a potent source of tensions and conflict in South Asia and, in a manner of speaking, Kashmir quintessentially represents a territorial dispute of massive dimensions, which remains unresolved and could be the cause of conflict between India and Pakistan. So does Siachen, and the absence of any agreement about delineation of the border in this area has led to a confrontation between the armed forces of the two countries that has occasioned a great deal of expense in terms of finance and lives lost to the extreme climatic conditions on the glacier. Lesser territorial disputes have obtained between South Asian countries focussing upon the Kachativu and Moore island controversies, or relating to the demarcation of naval boundaries in the Sir Creek between India and Pakistan, or in the Bay of Bengal between India and Bangladesh, but have a limited potential to ignite inter-State conflict.

The growth in ethnic-consciousness and resultant tensions in South Asia are of greater consequence, and could be placed within a theoretical construct, as being occasioned by the zeitgeist, which favours the assertion of sub-national particularities withn domestic polities. The spread of democratic forms of governance gives strength to ethnicity. Similarly, the rise of religious fundamentalism as part of a global phenomenon, would heighten this sense of ethnic particularity. These aspects of current international developments are apparent withn South Asia, in ethno-political movements ranging from Sindh to Kashmir/Punjab/Assam to the Chittagong Hill Tracts to the Tamil majority areas in Sri Lanka. In the historical perspective these entho-political movements represent the disintegrative processes that have traditionally affected the integrity of political structures in South Asia. It provides a powerful rationale for the SAARC modelity to enable an integrative process take shape in the region that would preserve the structure of the various nation-States by submerging their sub-national ethnicity in a larger supra-national identity.

The danger to South Asian peace from this resurgence of ethno-nationalism and inter-State conflicts ensuing therefrom springs from these which impinges on the latter's political economy. This occurred most recently with the ethnic Tamil crisis in Sri Lanka, and its spillover into Tamilnadu, which created its own political dynamics for the Indian federal system. More generally, ethno-political movements in one South Asian country can spill over its borders and adversely influence the politics, apart from the economy of the neighbouring country. This calls for greater inter-State cooperation in the resolution of such problems. Else the possibility obtains that both countries involved would be embarked on a collision course as occurred in the crisis of 1971. It might be added that the instrumentality of militarily assisting a particular ethnic group to reach a favourable solution of its demands vis-a-vis the national government is fraught with unpredictable consequence, as India discovered following its deployment of the IPKF in Sri Lanka to bring peace and stability into the Tamil majority in Tamil province of Sri Lanka.

Inter-State population flows of migrants in search of a better way of life in a neighbouring country or as refugees also has the potential to endanger inter-State tensions and conflicts in South Asia. It is worth remarking that all such population flows have taken place into India over the decades following partition, that would include emigration from Nepal, Bangladesh, and most recently, Sri Lanka. Clearly, the population outflows from Nepal and Bangladesh have a nexus with the aspirations of the migrants to improve their socio-economic condition in India. It is unfortunate that such migrants do become socio-economic problems for the receiving country and can become the pawns of domestic politics by their mobilisation into vote-banks, as occurred with the East Bengal/Bangladesh migrants in the Indian states of West Bengal and Assam. After a process of time the indetification of migrants presents growing problems as India is discovering in its efforts to pushback Bangladesh entrants. This issue has polarised the national political arena with the BJP making the forced return of these migrants a major plank in its foreign policy agenda. Any attempt to evict large populations by force clearly has the potential to engender inter-State tensions and conflict.

A different situation arose with regard to the Tamil refugees fleeing Sri Lanka in the wake of the SLAF campaign against militant groups in the Tamil-majority areas of Sri Lanka. Fortunately, the 1,000,000-1,50,000 Tamil refugees that still remain in India are being repatriated in terms of an agreement reached between the two countries. Earlier, the conflict potential of the fleeing Tamil refugees lay in the ethnic Tamil problem in Sri Lanka political issue in Tamilnadu leading to competitive jingoism by regional parties demanding the use of force to settle the issue. Further, this question became an issue in Centre-State relations. A similar problem of population outflows, and related to ethno-political tensions, is occurring with the ouster of the Nepali-origin population from Bhutan, and Chakmas from the Chittagong Hill Tracts. Any possible solution to stem these outflows, whether they are natural or forced, would require bilateral negotiations between the countries affected to contain the influx. The question does arise as to what should be done if these efforts fail.

The empirical evidence would suggest, however, that external intervention into Intra-State ethno-political and/or migratory issues could produce wholly unitended effects for the intervening power. India's utilisation of the Tamil militants has lever to resolve the ethinic crisis in Sri Lanka has resulted in a marked deterioration in the law and order situation in Tamilnadu and, to an extent, in other South Indian States. They are believed to have been used by political parties in Tamilnadu to further their electoral prospects. A similar entree of the Afghan mujahideen into the body politic of Pakistan ensued following their utilisation to serve Pakistan's foreign policy interests by assisting the American strategy of arming the mujahideen to wage war against the occupying Soviet forces in Afghanistan. Pakistan is now left with an excerbation of its law order problem and the establishment of a Klashnikov culture in the country. The empirical evidence strengthens the need therefore for South Asian countries to seriously discuss this new set of issues because they have the inherent potential to destabilise border areas in the region.

Any process of bilateral or multilateral dialogues within the South Asian region needs to appreciate the reality that serious political differences exist between them, that hinders the possibilities of greater cooperation in the sub-continent. These differences cannot be wished away and need to be firmly brought on the agenda for discussion and the search for solutions. The other reality which cannot be wished away is the looming (hegemonic) image of India. No doubt, India must understand the right of the South Asian countries to be apprehensive about it; but is equally the obligation of the other regional countries to appreciate the assurances given by India. There remains the question of underlying doubts and suspicions, which points again to the relevance of the SAARC forms to articulate apprehensions, and declare reassurances.

More specific measures can be suggested to further these objectives:

(1) Regular intervention in the public debate through all media forms to engender a greater awareness of how the existing and newer sources of tensions and conflicts are bedeviling the region, affecting the developmental process and, at one remove, subverting the processes of democratic governance.

(2) Highlight in public forums the value of multiateral/ bilateral dialogue between South Asian countries and the SAARC process, to erode tensions in the region. Apart from suggesting newer cooperative instrumentalities for this purpose, the existing agreements reached by SARRC, but lie dormant, like the Terrorism Convention and Agreement on Narcotic Drugs/Psychotropic Substances need being recognised as steps requiring vigorous implementation to clear the regional atmosphere of lurking doubts and suspicions

(3) The appreciation could also be underscored that certain natural channels of commerce have traditionally obtained in South Asia, and artificial barriers in their way have only succeeded in directing them into informal and illegal routes. This is occurring with regard to trade via third countries, that is within the knowledge of the countries concerned; hence the need to make overt what is the obtaining reallity. Besides trade these natural channels of commerce would include both capital and labour flows that need to be freed. The logic of commerce points to South Asia developing into a common market. The politics of the region will not permit this dispensation at present, but the strategic direction required might be recognised more clearly.

(4) Academic needs to be more greatly sensitised to the

need for undertaking conflict resolution studies relating to the South Asia, pertaining especially to ethno-political and migration issues in the region, which seems destined to become significant in future. It would serve this purpose admirably if joint studies were undertaken by scholars belonging to the countries affected by these problems, as is being attempted by the newly established Regional Centre for Strategic Studies. Furthermore, the possibility of establishing positions for visiting scholars in the prestigious institutions represented in the South Asian Dialogue to undertake such studies could be another modus to achieving this end.

The Second South Asian Dialogue of 1992 had emphasised the need for stabilisation and structural adjustment in the countries of the South Asian region, particularly in the context of the changing global scenario. Emphasising that the agenda for economic reforms should be defined domestically, the Indian experience was extensively discussed and analysed for possible lessons in economic policy making for other countries of the region.

An active domestic debate on the various policy options and an emerging consensus were seen as key ingredients for the success of the economic policy reforms within a democratic polity.

Against the background of this discussion, the developments in policy making and economic performance in India during the last year are sketched out here with a view to updating the record. This is followed by a broader discussion of the nature of regional co-operation and economic integration required to bring about the overall development of the countries of the South Asian region.

The nuclear dimension

The obtaining nuclear overhang in South Asia can now be discussed. The Report on Regional Non-Proliferation in South Asia submitted by the White House to the U.S. Congress in May holds that India and Pakistan have established the capability to manufacture nuclear weapons at short notice and also prossess credible means of delivery to attack value targets. This conclusion is in line with independent Russian assessments. Estimates of the nuclear capabilities available to the two countries have also been made by several organisations based on the quantities of fissile material believed to be in their possession. India and Pakistan are, uniquely, the only adversary but cryptonuclear powers in the world. There are other unique aspects of the nuclear situation in South Asia. India's present policy of keeping its option open which, incidentally, seems to have informed Pakistan, without either expressing or foreclosing that option is singular in the so-called non-proliferation regime.This policy enjoys wide domestic support in the two countries, but it also needs greater appreciation that they could only possess crude fission devices with their means of delivery premised on aircraft. It would require a series of tests to miniaturise nuclear warheads and gain assurance about the reliability/accuracy of their missiles, apart from the political/military leadership acquiring confidence that such last-resort weapons will function when they need to be utilised.

Despite these technological constraints there is a considerable body of opinion which holds that the present ambiguous nuclear situation in south Asia has led to a stabilisation of the mutual relationship. Witness the caution displayed by the armed forces of the two countries and their political leaderships during the various crises in relations during the last few years, e.g., Brasstacks Exercise (1987), Kashmir-related escalation of border tensions (1990), and the recent (1992-93) attempts by JKDA activists to violate the Line of Control. There are contrary arguments to suggest that availability of nuclear weapons at short notice constitutes a dangerous situation, with the likelihood of a nuclear exchange being triggered by inadvertence, if not design, and being occasioned by an escalation of conflict from the conventional level. It could, however, be argued that this entire question is somewhat irrelevant, since the primary threat to India arises from ethno-political and other domestic tensions in the polity, which can be inflamed by external powers intervention, and the nuclear weapons provide no defence against this range of problems. It might be further added that the economic costs involved would constrain any overt deployment of nuclear forces. These economic costs would not merely involve the expenses, incidentally, on establishing a nuclear force which, in the case of India, most address the presence of a nuclear China on its security horizons, but also the likelihood of bilateral/multilateral financial assistance getting prejudiced by such proliferation actions.

A word about the present state of the non-proliferation regime. There is optimism about its growing acceptability by events like the accession of France, China and South Africa to the UNP, Argentina and Brazil agreeing to a system of mutual inspection of their sensitive nuclear facilities, signing of major arms control agreements like START-I and START-II, withdrawal of tactical nuclear missles by the U.S., Russia and U.K., and moratoria placed by these nuclear weapons powers on nuclear testing and so an. At the same time, developments in the former Republics of the Soviet Union must cause the most profound concern. All tactical nuclear weapons have reportedly been shifted into Russia. There is no assurance, however, that fissile material, nuclear cores, if not entire nuclear weapons, are fully accounted for. Indeed, materials accounting procedures in the erstwhile Soviet Union were neither detailed nor strict because the nature of its political system permitted confidence that theft or misappropriation of such materials were not possible and could be easily detected. No such confidence is presently available with the break-up of the Soviet Union and the autonomy of its former Republics. The possibility of fissile materials, nuclear cores, if not entire nuclear weapons, remaining unaccounted for is real, and points to the extraordinary-danger of their falling into the hands of nuclear aspirants. There is besides newer problem accosting the non-proliferation regime after South Africa's self-confessedly admitting to making and, thereafter, dismantling six nuclear weapons. There can be no assurance that all its nuclear weapons have been uncovered and/or the fissile materials to produce a further number have been satisfactorily accounted for North Korea has highlighted the escape route available to NTP-signatories to withdraw from the Treaty whenever they chose; Iraq has revealed the clandestine path to the nuclear capabilities. These developments must be construed as adverse to the non-proliferation regime's containment.

The foregoing discussion provides the backdrop against which proposals for controlling, limiting and eventually eliminating nuclear weapons from the region must be considered. This parallels the American objective to "cap, then over the time, reduce, and finally eliminate the possession of weapons of mass destruction and their means of delivery" in South Asia. The technical implications of this measure would require ceasing production of fissile materials and work relating to missiles. It would also require that imports of materials, equipment or tecnnology that could further the military nuclear or missile programme should be stopped. Equity demands that all such proposals should be universal and non-discriminatory. Restricting these proposals to particular regions does not address the true nature or dimensions of the non-proliferation problem, especially in a milieu wherein the dilemma of fissile materials, nuclear cores/weapons/technology, apart from unemployed nuclear scientists and engineers, seeping out of the erstwhile Soviet Union and becoming available to nuclear aspirants has not been credibly resolved. There is, besides, the related dilemma of defining regions. In India's security perceptions the region must include China for the purpose of evolving any methodologies to control, reduce and eliminate nuclear weapons from South Asia.

There remains, however, the question of managing the nuclear situation in South Asia and, in particular, the crypto-nuclear adversarial relationship between India and Pakistan. The various confidence-building and tension-reducing proposals that could build upon existing arms control/confidence-building agreements in the nuclear and conventional areas, could comprise the following:

(1) Extending the agreement not to attack each other's identified nuclear facilities and installations to designated population and high value economic assets;

(2) The "hot-line" communications between the military leaderships could be extended to the political leaderships at the highest levels and upgraded with multiple-redundancy linkages to permit fail-safe communications at all times. This becomes of extreme importance in the ambiguous state of the nuclear relationships;

(3) Periodic meetings of military officials could be formalised into regular meetings at fixed intervals to sort out subsisting border problems, apart from ad-

hoc flag meetings to settle local dispute between field commanders;

(4) The agreement for providing advance information troop movements/military exercises could be widened to include deployments of offensive weapons systems like tanks, combat aircraft, and surface-to-surface missiles within specified border zones to reduce the likelihood of surprise attacks, apart from allowing military observers to be associated with field exercises;

(5) Similarly, the agreement to prevent violations of air space could be broadened to an "open skies" arrangement that would permit aerial reconnaissance of the specified border zones to be mutually undertaken for gaining confidence that no unwarranted military movements and force re-deployments were taking place.

There are further confidence-building measures at the declaratory level that could be considered for unilateral action like no-first-use pledges, no-nuclear-test declarations, promises to adhere to the guidelines of the Nuclear Suppliers Group and the Missile Technology Control Regime, besides innovative measures like sharing information on the location of strike corps elements, and so on.

It would, indeed, be advancing a counsel of perfection to suggest that all these measures are subsumed within the need to normalise bilateral relations between India and Pakistan. One pathway for proceeding purposively here would be to widen people-to-people contacts by meetings at various levels between academicians, journalists, professional and business groups, and increasing the two-way flow of information through various media channels, apart from bilateral trade via formal ageements. In short, the measures enuisaged in Article III of the Shimla Agreement need to be seriously implemented.

At the official level, however, the need for dialogue between the two countries cannot be over-emphasised and this must be extended to the nuclear dimension. Indeed the gaps in understanding and the dangerous consequences of misunderstandings stand accentuated by frequent statements made by Pakistan's leadership about their nuclear prowess and India's reticence in this regard. Why such inflamatory rhetoric is deemed necessary could be considered in this dialogue. There is besides the impermissible actions that could lead to an overt expression of nuclear capabilities, the peronage(s) designated to exercise release authority and so on. The nuclear game has it own rules and nuclear weapons possess their own intrinsic logic. Consequently, these measures, that were found necessary by the existing nuclear weapons powers, cannot be inapplicable to crypto-nuclear powers. Hence the need to address these basic issues relating to the military atom within the structure of an Indo-Pak dialogue.

There are different strands in Indo-Pak relations that give rise to cautious optimism in the possibilities of their betterment, which includes the signficant confidence-building measures that have been reached between them, and have been detailed above. some cause for greater optimism is possible from the manner in which the JKDA attempts to cross the Line of Control had been prevented with firmness by the Pakistan army but, more importantly, in close collaboration with the Indian army. This reinforces the belief that major crises in Indo-Pak relations like the Brasstacks affair and build-up of tensions in 1990 were handled by both countries with considerable adroitness and maturity. These sensibilities lie dormant presently, but are available to address the larger issues of adversarial Indo-Pak relations, if the political will could be generated on both sides.

Dimensions of inter-state conflict: the Indo-Pak case

Moving to the sources of inter-State tensions and conflicts in South Asia, and ways to mitigate them, it requires early recognition that the spirit of detente has not struck roots yet in the region. Neither has the example of neighbouring ASEAN, which shares many geo-political similarities with South Asia, like the preponderance of Indonesia in the region, established a standard for emulation by SAARC. We might question here ingrained beliefs that the dominance of India over the South Asian polity is the chief reason for concern, and the major impediment to its greater integration. Admittedly, India is the focus of the foreign policies of the smaller nations in the sub-continent some further reflection, however, on the causes for tensions and conflicts in the region would isolate the Indo-Pak contention, which possesses historical, political, religious and geo-strategic dimensions, and has now acquired a worrisome nuclear dimension. This needs to be discussed at greater length.

Kashmir

This would not be the place to detail the entire gamut of Indo-Pak disputes that have emerged since their independence, but we may identify the Kashmir issue as the principal contention between them that could escalate to armed conflict. The relative merits of the case pesented over the years by India and Pakistan to press their claims are too well-known to bear reiteration. The danger from the continuance of the Kashmir issue arises from its latent possibility of triggering violence, and it bears recognition that Kashmir has been either the cause or the chief theater of conflict between the two countries in the past Indo-Pak wars. A low intensity conflict proceeds at present in Kashmir, which has its roots in the partition of the country and certain errors made by India in the past. It cannot be the case, nevertheless, that external intervention by the provision of moral and material assistance and sanctuaries to Kashmiri militants would help in evolving a solution. Beliefs, morever, that the low intensity conflict in Kashmir would become India's Spanish ulcer do not acknowledge that India cannot abandon Kashmir to be either integrated within Pakistan or become an independent state. Any such action would raise several contentious questions, and, more significantly, the reliquishment of a Muslim-majority area would have serious repercussions for India's secular polity and might lead to extensive communal violence engineered by nationalistfundamentalist forces in the country.

It must be conceded that Pakistan also has a national position on Kashmir. A serious dialogue would seem to be the only way out, and, perhaps, by recognition of the Line of Control as the de jure division of the historical State of Kashmir. Of course, dialogues with the indigenous populations of the historical state of Jammu and Kashmir, and of the different regions comprising it, are essential as well, and matters like the sequencing of all these dialogues will also have to be considered at the proper time. But an over-riding necessity is that the leaders and peoples of India and Pakistan should realise that non-resolution of the Kashmir issue is bleeding both the countries by their common need to station large forces in this area, and their requirement for large armed forces to be maintained, equipped, modernised and expanded due to the prevailing atmosphere of tensions in the bilateral relationship.

Even if it was argued that India's other security concerns warrant periodical upgradations of its armed forces, it might be appreciated that a major portion of its military expenditure is designed against the threat assessed from Pakistan, whilst the security threat from China is reducing, and might largely recede as the recently-signed peace and tranquility agreement. Expenditures being incurred by India and Pakistan deriving, from their adversarial relationship, bear significant opportunity costs in terms of development outlays otherwise possible. A compromise on the Kashmir issue, preceded by a disengagement in Siachen, would permit the relationship to develop within more normal channels of international behaviour, and erode the most prescient cause for inter-State conflict in the sub-continent.

The international context

This focus on the Kashmir issue might be enlarged now to consider it within the larger international context, and the peace dividend promised by the end of the Cold War. The spirit of detente apparent in the international system has permitted various stubborn regional conflict situations being addressed towards evolving a solution eg., Cambodia, Namibia and Cyprus, the long-outstanding problem of apartheid in South Africa and enfranchisement of its black population is on the way to resolution. Of particular relevance to the Indo-Pak adversarial situation is the agreement signed between the PLO and Israel to usher peace into the most disputed area in the world. The conflict between them involved disputed territory and contention between opposed ideologies viz., nationalism and Zionism.

The rhetoric on both sides had traditionally argued for maximalist solutions to the problem e.g., refusing to accept ground realities like the entity of Israel (PLO), and the recognition of the Palestinians as a people (Israel). Assuredly, there will be many difficulties in translating the different steps envisaged in the peace agreement into political action, and there are powerful domestic constituencies that firmly oppose the agreement and would make strenuous efforts to obstruct its fruition. But, the significance of this momentous first step to bring peace into the Middle-East cannot be minimised, nor its promise disregarded, to resolve a most obstinate regional security problem. Without straining the simile too greatly there are important lessons in this event for India and Pakistan. First, that compromise in long-held maximalist positions in regional disputes is essential to break from sterile unproductive controversies. Second, there is wisdom in not seeking outside intervention, but not rejecting it either to promote the principle of bilateralism in Indo-Pak relations. Third, there would be value in quiet, low-profile discussions, perhaps in another country between duly accredited representatives of India and Pakistan to find solutions. Fourth, and this is central to the exercise, the realisation must dawn, as it did with the PLO/Isreal, that it was not possible for them to destroy each other and, therefore, necessity requires seeking the path of reconciliation.

National budgets, including defence allocations, are under considerable strain in India and Pakistan. The two defence establishments are, besides, finding it progressively more difficult to maintain the operational status of their weapon systems due to problems in arranging for their maintenance, spares and ancillaries from their principal suppliers viz., Russia and the United States. These constraints might assist this process of realisation in the wisdom of reconciliation. It is also conceivable that an additional factor in promoting this realisation might be renewed pressures from the international community to compose the Kashmir issue specifically and Indo-Pak disputes generally. The recently negotiated agreement in the Middle-East highlights the value of quite diplomacy and a step-wise methodology to reach the ultimate objective, besides the possibility of transcending U.N. resolutions.

Western Europe

The process of continuing change in post-cold war Europe and in India's own external environment has provided an impetus for internsification of relations between India and countries of this region based on complementarity of interests and mutual benefit. India's historical and cultural interaction with Europe also provides a unique dimension that further serves to strengthen mutual understanding and affinities. Over a million persons of Indian origin live in Western Europe, a tenth of them Indian citizens. Both the European Commssion and individual members of the European Union evolved new strategies to strengthen political dialogue and economic relations with Asian countries, including India. This trend was compelmented by India's economic reforms and efforts to globalise the Indian economy.

India's trade with the EU countries increased by 20 per cent over the previous year to reach dollar 14.89 billion in 1993; this upward trend continued during 1994. Collectively the largest trading partners of India, the EU countries accounted for 30 per cent of India's exports and imports. Similar progress was registered on the investment front. The share of West European countries in FDI approvals went up from 20 per cent in 1993 to 30 per cent in 1994. Actual investment inflows from Western Europe since the launching of India's economic reforms in July 1991 comprised 31 per cent of total inflows. West European countries also continued to be a leading source of development assistance, technology and collaborations and joint ventures.

The new Cooperation Agreement between the Republic of India and the European Community on Partnership and Development came into effect on 1 August 1994. The 8th Session of the India-EC Joint Commission was held in Brussels in October 1994. The broad principles of a strategy for economic and development cooperation with the EU up to the year 2000 was agreed on, focussing on continued assistance from the EU to India's development efforts.

India's relations with Germary, India's leading economic partner in Europe, was given further impetus through the exchanges of high level visits during 1994-95. German Minister for Development Cooperation visited India in February 1994. The German Minister for Economics attended the 11th Session of the Indo-German Joint Commission held in New Delhi in April 1994. An Indian Parliamentary delegation led by the speaker of the Lok Sabha, visited Germany in June-July 1994 and interacted with a wide cross-section of German Parliamentarians and leaders of various political parties.

The Vice-Chancellor and Foreign Minister of Germany visited India in July 1994 accompanied by a high-level business delegation. He underlined the central position occupied by India in terms of Germany's "Asia Concept Policy" and stressed the importance attached by Germany to developing closer relations with India on the basis of partnership in political, economic and cultural fields. He also reaffirmed Germany's support for the resumption of Indo-Pak bilateral dialogue and welcomed India's policy of transparency on human rights. He expressed support for a permanent seat for India in the UN Security Council. The German business delegation accompanying him evinced keen interest in increasing their presence in the Indian market through investments, particularly in the fields of power, chemicals and transportation infrastructure.

The Indo-German-Consultative Groups, which has emerged as a strong catalytic force in Indo-German reactions, held its Third Session in Bonn in August and submitted recommendations covering bilateral cooperation in political, economic, scientific, cultural and media fields.

Prime Minister paid a visit to the UK in March 1994. The visit marked a new era of relations between the UK and India, reinforcing trends towards a long term partnership based on mutual confidence and trust, shared values and mutual benefit. A Bilateral Investment Protection Agreement was concluded with the UK during the visit.The Indo-British Partnership Initiative (IBPI), launched in January 1993, extended for another year, achieved major success in promoting awareness of opportunities for trade and investment opened up by India's economic reforms. Indo-British trade continued to register a high rate of growth during 1994. There were several exchanges of visits between India and UK during 1994-95. Instruments of ratification of the Indo-UK Bilateral Investment Protection Agreement were exchanged during British Foreign Secretary's visit to India in January 1995. During the year, a Commercial Office of the British High Commission was opened in Bangalore and a decision taken to establish a Consulate General of India in Glasgow.

A delegation of the French Senate led by President of the Senate Committee for Foreign Affairs and Defence visited India in February 1994. In a letter to the Prime Minister, the French Prime Minister Edouard Balladur affirmed the desire of the French Government to impart new momentum to Indo-French relations in the political, economic and cultural fields. French Foreign Minister visited India in April 1994. He expressed French resolve to intensify relations with India particularly in the economic field. From the Indin side Ministers for

Agriculture, External Affairs and Health and Family Welfare visited France.

President of the Italian Senate visited India in Februray 1994. Trade and economic relations with Italy, the fourth largest market for Indian exports to Europe, continued to expand. Commerce Minister visited Italy for the 11th meeting of the Indo-Italian joint Economic Committee. The Italian President paid a State visit to India in February 1995 coinciding with the participation of Italy as partner country in the Indian Engineering Trade Fair. A Memorandum of Understanding concerning cooperation in the field of defence equipment was concluded between India and Italy on 4 November 1994.

Minister of State for External Affairs paid official visit to Ireland and Spain in October 1994. The visits focussed on strengthening bilateral trade and economic relations with these countries. A partimentary delegation led by the Speaker of the Lok Sabha visited Ireland in July 1994. A Consulate General of Portugal was opened in Goa in April 1994 to promote Indo-Portugese relations in the areas of trade, tourism and culture. The 11th Session of the Indo-Swedish Joint Commission for Economic, Industrial, Technical and Scientific Cooperation was held in Stockholm in May 1994. The Indian delegation was led by Minister of State for Industry. The meeting provided impetus to trade and economic relations between India and Sweden.

Minister of State for Communications visited Denmark in May 1994. Ministers of State for Surface Transport and for Petroleum visited Norway. The Norwegian Minister for Development Cooperation visited India in May 1994. Official level consultations between India and Norway on economic, industrial and technicasl cooperation were held in New Delhi. Minister of State for Defence paid a visit to Greece in October 1994. The visit coincided with the first ever participation by India at the Defence Production Fair "Defendory" which was held in Athens in October 1994. Shri Mallikarjun's visit and India's participation in "Defendory" strengthened prospects for Indo-Greek cooperation in the field of defence production. In November 1994, protocols were concluded with the principality of Andorra establishing diplomatic and consular relations between India and Andorra. During 1994-95, double taxation avoidance agreements were conceded with Malta, Cyprus and Switzerland.

Eastern Europe

There was considerable interaction between India and the countries of the Commonwealth of Independent States (CIS) as well Central and Eastern Europe during 1994-95. With practically all these countries, India has had longstanding relations of friendship and cooperation based on trust and confidence. The evolution of these countries in direction of democratic pluralism and market-oriented economic structures has brought them closer to India in terms of basic orientation. India has established a mutually beneficial economic and commercial interation with all the countries in East Europe. Direct contacts between the Indian Parliament and the parliamentary systems in many of these countries are emerging as an important new dimension in the bilateral relationships.

India's relations with the Russian Federation are friendly and multifaceted, encompassing political consultation on matters of mutual interest, significant economic and commercial interation and cooperation in science and technology, defence, atomic energy, space, culture and education.

Prime Minister, Shri P.V. Narasimha Rao visited Russia from 29 June to 2 July 1994. He was accompanied by the Ministers for Commerce, Civil Aviation and Tourism, the Ministers of State in the Prime Minister's Office, and for External Affairs Shri R.L. Bhatia and senior officers. The Prime Minister had separate delegation level talks with President Yeltsin and Prime Minister Chernomyrdin. Deputy Prime Minister and Culture Minister called on the Prime Minister. The Prime Minister addressed a representative group of Parliamentarians from both Houses of Russian Parliament.

The visit ushered in a qualitatively new stage of Indo-Russian relations. The Moscow Declaration on the Protection of the interests of Pluralist States sets out the post-cold war challenges posed to the viability of large, multi-ethnic, multi-lingual, multi-cultural and multi-religious states by the forces of aggressive nationalism, religious and political extremism, terrorism and separatism and the need to combat these challenges thorugh democracy, tolerance, secularism and the rule of law. It is recognised as a unique document in international relations and has subsequently been circulated as a UN Document at the joint initiative of India and Russia. The Declaration on Further Development and Intensification of Bilateral Cooperation underlines the broad identity of views of the two countries on important regional and international issues, and identified priority areas and directions of cooperation between the two countries. In addition, Agreements and Protocols were signed on cooperation in tourism, environment, space, science and technology, standarsation and metallurgy. The 1992 Agreement on defence credit was extended for a further period of two years and an agreement on setting up of a joint venture in military aviation was signed. The first meeting of the co-chairmen of the Inter-Governmental Joint Commission, Indian Minister for Commerce and Russian Deputy Prime Minister was held in Delhi in June 1994. Priority areas of cooperation were identified and the Joint Commission held its first meeting in Moscow in September 1994. Nine Working Groups-on Trade and Economic Cooperation; Power and Non-Conventional Sources of Energy; Petroleum; Ferrous and Non-Ferrous Metallurgy; Science and Technology; Culture; Coal; Information Technology; and Environment-held meetings and identified their respective areas of cooperation.

The Home Minister visited Russia during August-September 1994. The visit gave a fresh impetus to bilateral cooperation, particularly in areas such as combating terrorism, organised crime and narcotics trafficking. Leader of Opporsition in Lok Sabha and Chairman of the Standing Committee on External Affairs headed a Parliamentary delegation to Russia in January 1995 and had a number of high level meetings.

A nine-member Parliamentary Delegation led by the Chairman visited India in November 1994 while the Russian Prime Minister VS Chernomyrdin visited India on 23 and 24 December 1994 along with a high level delegation. He had discussions with Prime Minister followed by delegation level talks and also called on President and Vice President. Eigth documents, including agreements in promotion of mutual protection of investment, shipping, exploration and peaceful uses of outer space, implementation of the programme of defence cooperation upto the year 2000 and purchases of commodities in India for the period 1995-97 were signed. During the year several rounds of Foreign Office Consultations were also held between the two countries.

Indo-Ukrainian relations were given direction and impetus by the visit of Foreign Minister Zlenko in April

1994. During the visit, three agreements were signed: Protocol of Consultations between the Minister of External Affairs of India and the Minister of Foreign Affairs of Ukraine; Agreement on the Inter-Government Joint Commission on Trade, Economic, Scientific, Technological, Industrial and Cultural Cooperation; and Agreement on Economic and Technical Cooperation. The first meeting of the Indo-Ukrainian Joint Commission and the Foreign Office Consultations were held in Kiev in December 1994.

The State visit by President Dr. Shanker Dayal Sharma from 26 to 29 May 1994 emphasied the importance India attached to relations with Bulgaria. The President had discussions with President Zhelev, addressed the Bulgarian National Assembly and was awarded an Honorary Doctorate by the University of Sofia. During the visit six Agreements on Quarantine and Plant Protection; Veterinary and Sanitary Agreement; Avoidance of Double Taxation; Combating Organised Crime, International Terrorism, Illegal Trafficking in Narcotics and Psychotropic Substances; Protocol on Foreign Office Consultation and Cooperation; Cooperation in Tourism–were signed and a Joint Statement was issued. Bulgarian Culture Minister paid an official visit to India during February-March 1994 and the Cultural Exchange Programme for 1994-96 was signed.

President Dr. Shankar Dayal Sharma paid a State visit to Romanian from 30 May to 2 June 1994. The President held discussions with President Iliescu; addressed the Joint Session of the Romanian Senate and the Chamber of Deputies; and received an Honorary Doctorate from the University of Bucharest. During the visit, an Agreement on Combating Organised Crime, International Terrorism, Illicit Trafficking in Narcotics and Psychotropic Substances and other Illegal Activities;

an Agreement on Cooperation in Tourism; a Declaration of Principles and Directions of Cooperation and the Cultural Exhchange Programme for 1994-96 were concluded.

President of the Republic of Poland Lech Walesa paid a State visit to India in March 1994. Delegation-level talks led by the Prime Minister on the Indian side and by President Walesa on the Polish side were held and were followed by a tele-a-tele between the two leaders. Minister of State for Defence visited Poland in June 1994 to discuss further prospects for cooperation in defence.

Hungarian Political State Secretary for Defence visited India in March 1994 and State Secretary for Foreign Affairs paid and official visit to New Delhi in September 1994. A Protocol on Foreign Office Consulations was signed during the visit. A Hungarian Parliamentary delegation led by the Speaker of the National Assembly visited India in November 1994.

Minister of State for Defence visited the Czech Republic in June 1994 and Foreign Secretary visited Prague on 9 August 1994. The Czech Republic upgraded its diplomatic representation in India to that of Ambassador Extraordinary and Plenipotentiary. The Joint Trade Committee on Economics, Trade and Technical Cooperation held its first meeting at Prague in January 1995.

Minister of State for Defence visited the Slovak Republic in June 1994. He called on Slovak President and Prime Minister and Foreign Minister. Prime Minister of the Slovak Republic, Jozeh Moravcik paid an official visit to India in June 1994. He called on the President, Vice President, and had talks with the Prime Minister and he also met Indian businessmen and industrialists. A Protocol on Foreign Office Consultations; a Memorandum of Understanding on Cooperation in

Science and Technology; and a Memorandum of Understanding concerning Indo-Slovak Joint Committee on Trade were also signed. It was also agreed to open a resident Indian Mission in Bratislava. The Union of Slovak Industry and CII also concluded a Memorandum of Understanding. The Slovak Republic upgraded its diplomatic representation in India to that of Ambassador Extraordinary and Plenipotentiary and also established an Honorary Consulate in Calcutta.

An Armenian delegation led by Minister of Science and Higher Education visited India in March 1994 and held discussions with Minister of State (Prime Minister's Office and Science and Technology). An Agreement on Cooperation in Science and Technology, a Memorandum of Understanding on concluding an Agreement on Economic and Technical Cooperation were signed. Armenia established its diplomatic representation in India by appointing an Honorary Consul. India has offered humanitarian assistance of medicine valued at Rs. five lakh to Armenia.

Deputy Prime Minister of Moldova paid an unofficial visit to New Delhi in May, 1994 and held discussions with Minister of State for External Affairs, Shri Salman Khurshid. A Lithuanian delegation led by the Minister of Energy visited India in March 1994. He held discussions with Minister of State for External Affairs, Shri R.L. Bhatia and senior officers in the Ministry of Power. Lithuania established its Honorary Consulate in New Delhi in October 1994. India kept a close watch on the developments in the Former Yugoslavia, particularly the continuing criss in Bosnia-Herzegovina. India supports the efforts of the Interanational Conference on Former Yugoslavia, basically because to-date it is the only attempt at finding a settlement that is based on regard for legitimate aspirations and interests of all parties to the conflict.

India recognised Bosnia-Herzegovina on 11 May 1992 along with the Republic of Croatia and Slovenia but not as a Muslim State.

India's Ambassador to Croatia, presented his credentials in June 1994. Commerce Minister visited Croatia on 17 September 1994. An Agreement on Trade and Economic Cooperation was signed during the visit and the Croation Assistant Minister of Economic Affairs led a delegation to India in November 1994 during the India International Trade Fair.

The Americas

The year 1994-95 witnessed rapid and diversified growth in the Indo-US relations following Prime Minister's visit to the USA from 14 to 20 May 1994. Prime Minister Shri P.V. Narasimha Rao and President Clinton promised to cooperate in the search for solutions to global challenges posed by weapons of mass destruction, AIDS, environmental degradation, population growth, poverty, international terrorism and narcotics trafficking. Agreement was also reached to expand the pace and scope of high level exchanges on the full range of political, economic, commercial, scientific, technological and social issues. The two leaders agreed to seek ways to expand their cooperation at the United Nations. Two Memoranda of Understanding-on Cooperation Measures to Increase Awareness and Support for Efforts to Combat Production, Distribution and Use of Illegal Drugs and on Planning, Conservation and Management of Natural and Cultural Heritage Sites-were also signed.

Commercial and economic interaction remained the most vital sector of Indo-US cooperation through 1994-95. Bilateral trade in 1993 equalled US dollar 7.3 billion with a trade surplus of US dollar 1.8 billion in India's favour. The USA remained the single largest investor-country in terms of direct foreign investment in India, with approved investments from the US between January to September 1994 amounting to Rs. 14,302 million. Actual FDI inflows from the USA from 1991 to September 1994 amounted to Rs. 2,039 million. US Energy Secretary visited India in July 1994 leading a large Presidential Mission when four joint statements were signed and 11 cooperative projects between private companies of the two countries were announced. US Commerce Secretary led a Presidential Business Development Mission to India in January 1995 and during the visit the two countries signed a Memorandum of Understanding setting up the Indo-US Commercial Alliance.

Minister of Power visited USA in November 1994. Several agreements were signed during the visit. Minister of State for Non-Conventional Energy Sources visited the USA in December and a number of Memoranda of Understanding for cooperation between Indian and the US institutions/firms were signed during the visit. Air Chief Marshal visited US in August 1994 while Chief of Army Staff visited in September 1994. The second round of talks on a new Indo-US Extradition Treaty was held in Washington in October 1994.

Democrat Congressmen Gary L Ackerman, Jim MC Dermott accompanied by Congresswoman Barbara-Rose Collins visited India in November 1994 while Commander-in-Chief of the US Pacific Command visited India in December 1994. In September 1994, the Indian and US Navies conducted a joint Special Operations exercise at Ratnagiri (Mirya Bay). Defence Secretary visited India in January 1995 and an Agreed Minute on Defence Relations between India and the USA was signed. It was agreed that growth of bilateral defence relations would be evolutionary and related to convergence on global and regional issues.

India and the US held a further round of discussions

on non-proliferation regional security and disarmament in London in April 1994. The two countries also agreed to intensity cooperative efforts to achieve a Comprehensive Test Ban Treaty (CTBT) and a verifiable global ban on the production of fissible material for nuclear weapons purposes. US pronouncements on the human rights situations in India gave rise to considerable misunderstanding. Differences in perception continued over Pakistan's support to terrorism. However, the situation improved later in the year as a result of greater restraint and objectivity exercised by US authorities.

Indo-Canadian relations witnessed greater interation, especially in the economic and commercial spheres. From January to September 1994, foreign direct investment approvals for Canada amounted to Rs. 417 million as against the total Canadian investment approvals for 1993 of Rs. 300 million. Canadian imports from India during January to May 1994 totalled Canadian dollar 178 million, registering an increase of 30.5 per cent as compared to the imports during the same period last year. Canadian exports to India during January to May 1994 registered a marginal increase of 5.1 per cent as compared to the same period last year. The Canadian Minister for International Trade accompanied by a large Canadian business delegation visited India in October 1994. Home Minister visited Canada in October 1994 and Mutual Legal Assistance Treaty on combating terrorism, drug trafficking and organised crime was signed during the visit.

India maintains very good relations with all the Latin American and Caribbean countries. During 1994-95, India's relations with these countries were consolidated by several exchanges of high level visits, joint commission meetings and contacts at various levels. The Foreign Minister and Minister of Environment of Brazil also visited India. Minister of Civil Aviation and Tourism visited Brazil and discussed various means of close cooperation in tourism. Minister of Textiles, Deputy Minister for Education also visited Brazil in 1994, the latter to participate in the Conference on 'Education for All.'

A three-member delegation led by Minister of Parliamentary Affairs attended the inauguration ceremonies of the new President of Mexico. President Dr. Carlos Saul Menem of Argentina visited India in March 1994 to take over Chairmanship of G-15 and extended his stay to pay a bilateral visit. The leaders of India and Argentina discussed important international issues and matters of bilateral importance. Several agreements on bilateral cooperation were signed during the visit. Minister of Civil Aviation and Tourism visited Argentina in June 1994 to promote tourist traffic from South America to India and Minister of Communications visited Buenos Aires during March 1994 to attend the first World Telecommunication Development Conference organised by the ITU. The then Chief Justice of India visited Buenos Aires in August 1994 as the leader of the Indian delegation to the International Law Association Congress. The Embassy in Bogota which was closed down in 1993 was reopened in October 1994. Both India and Colombia have expressed a desire to have close cooperation and similarity of views in relations to the Non-Aligned Movement and the next Summit. Venezauelan Minister of State for Foreign Trade participated in the G-15 Conference held in New Delhi March 1994. Minister for Legal Affairs of Jamaica participated in the G-15 Conference held in New Delhi in March 1994. During the year, a few Indian companies signed Memoranda of Understanding with Guyanese companies for establishment of joint ventures, ITPO participated in the international fair, EXPOCOMER' 94, held in Panama and diplomatic relations were established with Honduras.

Vice President and Foreign Minister of Suriname, where 40 per cent of the population is of India origin, paid a State visit to India during November 1994 and held bilateral discussions with Indian leaders. India agreed to donate an agricultural project, a home gardening project and 10,000 bicycles to Suriname. The first Joint Commission meeting between India and Suriname was held in November 1994.

APEC organised a buyer-seller meet in May 1994 in Chile. Supreme Court Justice Kuldip Singh and Delhi High Court Justice Y.K. Sabharwal visited Chile in August 1994 to attend the post-meet of the International Law Conference.

Minister of Planning and Development of Trinidad and Tobago visited India and discussed matters of bilateral interest with Indian leaders. Government of Trinidad and Tobago has given five acres of land on a 99-year lease to Government of India for setting up Mahatma Gandhi Institute for Cultural Cooperation. ITPO arranged participation of 19 firms at the third International Exposition 94, held in Port of Spain in April 1994.

Cuban Foreign Minister visited India in March 1994 and held discussions with Indian leaders on ways of expanding bilateral cooperation and trade. Minister of State for Non-Conventional Energy Sources visited Cuba in June 1994 to attend Solar Energy International Conference. India has donated a 11 kw solar energy plant to Cuba to electrify a village. Minister of State for Commerce led the Indian delegation to the second session of the Indo-Cuban Joint Commission held in June-July 1994 in Havana. A four-member delegation from Cuba visited India for exploring possibilities of import of sugar mill machinery and spares from India.

Africa (South of The Sahara)

India enjoys warm relations with the African countries and has always attached special significance to her relations with Africa. Africa continues to be a major thrust area under the Indian Technical and Economic Cooperation (ITEC) and Special Commonwealth African Assistance Programme (SCAAP), executed by the Ministry of External Affairs. Out of a total of 1,350 slots allocated for training in Indian civilian institutions under ITEC for 1994-95, 768 (more than 50 per cent) were reserved for countries in Africa. Twenty-eight Indian experts are also in station in various African countries as of December 1994. Out of 250 slots offered to friendly developing countries for training in Indian defence establishments under the ITEC Programme, more than 150 were allotted to countries in Africa.

The changed politicl scenario in Southern Africa, the integration of South African and Namibian economies, the entry of South Africa into Southern Africa Development Community (SADC), the revival of the Eastern Africa Community among Kenya, Tanzania and Uganda, and greater cooperation among countries of the southern and eastern regions are positive developments and could be expected to play a vital role in the economic regeneration and development of Africa.

Vice President, Shri K.R. Narayanan accompanied by Smt. Usha Narayanan, Smt. Sonia Gandhi and Minister of State for Commerce, represented India at the inauguration of Dr. Mandela as the first President of the new South Africa. Dr. Mandela paid a State visit to India January 1995 and was the Chief Guest at the Republic Day celebrations. During his visit, India and South Africa signed a Treaty on Principles of Inter-State Relations and Cooperation, an Agreement to set up a Joint Commission and a Protocol providing for regular consultations between the Foreign Ministries of the two countries. The Indian Emabssy established in Pretoria in May 1994 was redesignated as High Commission with South Africa joining the Commonwealth on 1 June 1994. India also established a Consulate General in Durban in May 1994, and the Indian Cultural Centre in Johannesburg was converted into a Consulate General Indexpo '94, the largest single country trade exhibition ever organised in South Africa was held in Johannesburg in August 1994. The Indian naval ships, *INS Gomati* and *INS Khukri* visited Durban and Simonstown in December. The South African Deputy Foreign Minister visited India in November 1994. A bilateral agreement to set up the India-South Africa Joint Commission and a Protocol providing for regular consultations between the Foreign Offices were initialled.

During the visit of President Mugabe in March 1994, India agreed to cooperate with Zimbabwe in the informal sector particularly in the development of small and middle enterprises. Smt. Sonia Gandhi attended the ceremony to mark the reintegration of Walvis Bay and the off-shore Islands into Namibia as Special Guest of President Sam Nujoma. A Namibian Parliamentary delegation led by the Chairman of the National Council visited India in September 1994 followed by Defence Minister for purchase of defence equipment. The visit of Finance and Communication Minister of Seychelles in January 1994 has raised hopes of improved trade relations between India and Seychelles. Two Indian navalships-*INS Gomati* and *INS Khukri*-paid a goodwill visit to Port Victoria from 23 to 26 November 1994. India deputed seven experts to Seychelles under the ITEC Programme.

Following the death of President Juvenal Habyarimana of Rwanda in an air crash on 6 April 1994 and the outbreak of ethnic violence in that country, all the

Indians there (300 in number) migrated. India supplied relief materials worth Rs. five lakh to Rwandese refugees in Tanzania. An Indian army battalion to United Nations Aid Mission in Rwanda (UNAMIR) reached Kigali on 10 Novermber 1994. Rwanda has shown interest in increasing and strengthening economic and technical cooperation with India. The Angolan External Affairs Minister paid an official visit to India in April 1994. Compaore, President of Burkino Faso paid a visit to India in July 1994. India announced a grant of Rs. 15 crore approximately for setting up an agricultural development project in Burkina Faso.

The traditionally close and friendly relations between Mauritius and India have deepened further during 1994-95. Vice President leading a high-level delegation visited Mauritius for one day in May 1994. Other visits included those of Mauritian Vice President, and Ministers of External Affairs and Finance. Bilateral trade has increased by almost 30 per cent in 1994 and a number of new joint ventures in different fields were established. Mauritius has emerged as the main centre for channelising investments into India through off-shore funds as a result of the advantageous provisions of the treaty for Avoidance of Double Taxation. Twenty-nine civilian training slots were utilised by Mauritius under the ITEC Programme during the year.

Indo-Kenyan relations continued to be warm and friendly, characterised by mutual regard. President Moi stopped over in Delhi on his way to Beijing in May 1994. India donated 476 metric tonnes of rice to Kenya for the drought-affected areas. A Cultural Exchange Programme was signed between the two nations in May 1994. Minister of Civil Aviation and Tourism visited Tanzania in January 1994 and the Tanzanian Home Minister-cum-Deputy Prime Minister visited India. Tanzania utilised 23 civilian training slots under the ITEC Programme. India's relations with Uganda witnessed positive developments during 1994-95. President Museveni led a high-powered trade and investment delegation to India in September 1994. In December, Ugandan Minister of Education and Sports visited India while several Indian business delegations visited Uganda.

General Gnassingbe Eyadema, President of Togo, paid a State visit to India in September 1994. This opened a new chapter in mutual relations and added an impetus to bilateral cooperation between the two countries. India also announced a grant of Rs. 10 crore approximately for setting up of an agricultural project in Togo and agreed to cooperate in the fields of city transportation, healthcare, scientific research, trade, industry and agriculture. India and Togo also decided to set up a Joint Commission and signed a Memorandum of Understanding on Economic and Technical Cooperation. General Sani Abacha, Head of State of Nigeria visited India in March-April 1994 to attend G-15 Summit and also held bilateral discussions with Indian leadership. Nigeria utilised 10 civilian training slots under the ITEC Programme during 1994-95.

President Diouf of Senegal visited New Delhi in March 1994 to attend the G-15 Summit and had wide-ranging bilateral discussions with the Prime Minister. Foreign Minister also attended the G-15 Troika and Ministerial level meetings. An eye clinic in Ghana is under execution by India. Ghana utilised 13 civilian training slots while two Indian experts were deputed there under ITEC Programme. In Mozambique, after decades of civil war, the ruling Frelimo Party and the main opposition Renamo signed a Peace Accord in 1992 and participated in the country's first multi-party elections in October 1994 under UN supervision. Frelimo Party leader, Joaquin Chissano was re-elected as President. India welcomed this development.

East Asia

India-China relations in 1994-95 continued to improve steadily and to expand into new areas of cooperation. The momentum of high level political dialogue was maintained in 1994 to expand cooperation and create a favourable climate in which the two countries can work for the resolution of outstanding issues. There were several exchange of visits between China and India. The situation along the India-China border remained peaceful during the year. The seventh meeting of the India-China Joint Working Group (JWG) held in Beijing in July 1994 continued discussions on the boundary question and on the implementation of the Border Peace and Tranquility Agreement while the India-China Expert Group (EG) set up under the above Agreement held two meetings is February and April 1994. The two countries also agreed in principle to open more points for border trade and trade through Shipkila in Himachal Pradesh started on 16 July 1994. In the first nine months of 1994, the total volume of bilateral trade was US dollar 593 million, an increase of 29.5 per cent over the corresponding period last year. The Vice President during his visit to China in October 1994, emphasised the need to further increase cooperation in economic and scientific-technological fields and agreements in several fields were signed. The Festival of India was held in China during May and June 1994. The two countries also celebrated the fortieth anniversary of *Panchsheel* or the Five Principles of Peaceful Co-existence.

The economic and commercial relations between India and Japan continued to grow and Japan remained the largest bilateral donor of development assistance to India. It has pledged 1,25,765 million yen, approximately equivalent to Rs. 3,920 crore as ODA to India for 1994-95, a five per cent increase over the previous year. This year's ODA loan package comprises twelve projects covering power, transport, drinking water and sewage system, environment and afforestation sectors. The Japan International Cooperation Agency (JICA) conducted a feasibility study on the setting up of an Industrial Model Town in Haryana. India's trade with Japan during 1993-94 was Rs. 10,231.13 crore of which India's exports were worth Rs. 5,482.21 crore and imports were worth Rs. 4,748.92 crore. During April-July 1994 India's total trade with Japan was Rs. 3,636.22 crore, exports being Rs. 1,904.82 crore and imports being Rs. 1,731.40 crore. Japanese investors are showing considerable interest in the new economic policies of the Government of India.

India's relations with the Republic of Korea (ROK) continued to expand rapidly during 1994-95. The third round of Foreign Office Consultations was held in New Delhi on 6 April 1994 while the Union Minister for Surface Transport visited Seoul in October 1994 along with a delegation of the shipping sector that made series of useful presentations on investment attractions in India to major ROK business conglomerates such as Hyundai, Daewoo, Samsung, Hallu and Kookdang. DCM-Daewoo have agreed for a joint collaboration to produce passenger cars in India. The two-way trade betweeen India and ROK exceeded US dollar one billion for the first time in 1993. ROK's direct investment approvals to India by September 1994 amounted to Rs. 474.6 million. There were exchange of other visits between the two countries on various fields.

India maintained friendly relations with the Democratic People's Republic of Korea (DPRK) and India expressed profound sorrow and grief at the passing away of Kim II Sung on 8 July 1994. Bilareral consultations at Secretary-level were held on 23 March 1994 wherein important interantional issues and bilateral relations including economic cooperation and cultural exchange programme were discussed.

India enjoys a friendly relationship with Mongolia which was further cemented during 1994-95. President P Ochirbat paid a State visit to India in January 1994 when a Treaty of Friendly Relations and Cooperation was concluded, besides agreements on establishing a Joint Committee on Cooperation and on Avoidance of Double Taxation. Agriculture Minister and Commerce Minister visited Ulaan Baator during 1994. India participated in the fourth Mongolia Assistance Group meeting in Tokyo in November 1994. Chartered flights from India to Mongolia opened during 1994.

Central Asia

India is actively engaged in promoting her friendly relations with Central Asian countries as well as with Azerbaijan and Turkey. Minister of State for External Affairs, Shri Salman Khurshid led a delegation and had detailed discussions with the Kazakh leadership on international issues and bilateral relations. In August 1994, the new Foreign Minister of Kazakhastan had detailed discussions with Minister of State for External Affairs, Shri R.L. Bhatia in New Delhi, and their Defence Minister visited India in February 1995. Kazakh Airways has started regular commercial flights between Almaty and New Delhi and the Kazakh Chamber of Commerce and Industry has established a Joint Business Council with Federation of Indian Chambers of Commerce and Industry in November 1994.

The first Indian resident Ambassador to Kyrghystan credentials to President Askar Akaev in June 1994. Minister of State for External Affairs, Shri Salman Khurshid who visited Bishkek in June 1994 had discussions with the Kyrghyz leaders who welcomed greater Indian presence in Central Asia. India's relations with Tajikistan also received considerable stimulus with the visit of Minister of State for External Affairs, Shri

Salman Khurshid in June 1994. An Indo-Tajik credit Agreement for extension of an Indian credit line of US dollar five million was signed during the visit. The first resident Indian Ambassador in Dushanbe is in position since December 1994. The Tajik Government is presently represented in India by an Honorary Consul.

Bilateral relations between India and Uzbekistan are marked by close mutual understanding and support.The second sessio of the Indo-Uzbek Joint Commission was held on 22 November 1994 in India. An agreement was signed to use the second tranche of the US dollar 10 million credit which was announced by the Prime Minister during his visit to Uzbekistan in May 1993 after the finalisation of contracts for the first tranche. The Director of India Cultural Centre in Tashkent has been functioning since May 1994 and Doordarshan programmes are directly telecast there. Embassy of Uzbekistan has been upgraded to the level of Ambassador in September 1994 and India has a resident Ambassador in Ashgabat (Turkmenistan) since June 1994. Turkmenistan has opened a resident mission in New Delhi.

India has opened Consulate General in Istanbul and India's External Affairs Minister and some other dignitaries visited Turkey in 1994. The President of Turkey, Suleyman Demirel paid an official visit to India from 30 January to 2 February 1995 and had discussions with President, Prime Minister and other Indian leaders on cooperation in international fora and on bilateral cooperation in diverse fields. Agreements on tourism and avoidance of double taxation were signed during the visit.

The Gulf, West Asia and North Africa

Historically, India and the neighbouring Gulf region have a close interaction based on trade routes and Islam. In recent times, these ties have acquired a significant socio-economic dimension. Currently, India imports nearly two-thirds of her oil from this region and trade with the Gulf countries stood at over Rs. 20,206 crore in 1993-94 (Indian Exports: Rs. 6,260 crore; Indian imports: Rs. 13,946 crore). During this year total value of Indo-Gulf trade grew by 23 per cent. Over 20 lah Indian nationas are estimated to be living in these countries most of whom are gainfully employed. The inward annual remittances from these Indians through banking channels are currently estimated to be Rs. 7,800 crore. The Gulf region is one of the largest markets for the Indian exports. India has, therefore, consistently called for peace, stability and security in this region.

Indo-Bahrain relations continued to develop in various fields. A 22-member delegation of Bahrain Chambers of Commerce and Industries visited India in April 1994 and signed an agreement with FICCI for setting up a Joint Business Council.

Even as India's relations with Iraq have remained restricted by the UN economic sanctions on that country, there was gradual upgradation in bilateral contacts. India has consistently advocated phased lifting of the UN economic sanctions in tandem with Iraqi compliance with the terms of the relevant UN Security Council resolutions. Iraqi Foreign Minister visited India in April 1994 as Iraqi President's Special Envoy.

During 1994-95, Indo-Kuwait relations continued to be on the upswing. On a number of occasions, India reiterated her commitment to Kuwaiti independence, sovereignty and territorial integrity. The Minister of Communication, Electricity and Water of Kuwait and a 15-member Kuwati Multi-Disciplinary Economic delegation visited India during 1994 to explore possibities of boosting bilateral economic cooperation. Kuwaiti Oil

Minister paid an official visit in January 1995 and held extensive talks with Minister of State for Petroleum and Natural Gas for bilateral cooperation in oil sector.

The Minister of Chemicals and Fertilizers paid an official visit to Oman in July 1994 and a Memorandum of Understanding envisaging preparation of feasibility report for US dollar 900 million fertilizer joint venture was signed. The Omani Minister of State for Foreign Affairs paid an official visit to India in August. An Indo-Omani Agreement setting principal conditions of the long-term gas supply contract for the import of Omani natural gas through a pipeline across the Arabian Sea was signed in Muscat, Oman on 28 September 1994.

India endeavoured to strengthen economic-commercial relations with Qatar and has recently emerged as a major buyer of ammonia from Qatar. The Minister of State for External Affairs, Shri R.L. Bhatia visited Qatar in July 1994 called on the Amir and held extensive talks with his Qatari counterpart on regional issues and bilateral matters.

India's substantive ties with the kingdom of Saudi Arabia developed satisfactorily during 1994-95 with the bilateral trade reaching the record level of US dollar two billion. The Finance Minister led the Indian delegation for the Fourth Session of the Indo-Saudi Joint Commission held in Riyadh in December 1994 and had meetings with Saudi Ministers of Foreign Affairs, Oil, Finance and Commerce. He also addressed the members of Saudi Chambers of Commerce and Industry, who evinced great interest in economic ties with India.

India's multi-faceted relations with the United Arab Emirates (UAE) continued to grow during the year. In the UAE, a trade fair titled 'India in Dubai' was inaugurated by the Minister of Commerce in September 1994. Around 163 participants attended the fair and orders worth US dollar 55 million were booked. The Eighth Session of the Indo-UAE Joint Commission was held in Abu Dhabi in September.

India's relations with Yamen have been marked by friendship and cordiality. India had to evacuate around 1,700 Indian and some foreign nationals from Yemen. Ali Abdullah Saleh was re-elected as the President of the Republic of Yemen on 2 October. Abdo Rabbo Mansoor Hadi was appointed the new Vice President. Dr. Abdul Karim Iryani was appointed as Deputy Prime Minister of Foreign Affairs. The President, the Prime Minister and the Minister of External Affairs sent congratulatory messages to their newly appointed Yemeni counterparts.

Efforts to strengthen the bilateral relationship with Iran were further pursued during 1994-95 with exchange of high level bilateral visits. External Affairs Minister paid an official visit to Tehran in March 1994 to attend the Seventh Session of India-Iran Joint Commission. The Foreign Minister of Iran visited New Delhi in January 1995 in connection with the Eighth Session of the India-Iran Joint Commission. the Session reviewed the status of bilateral functional cooperation and gave directions for strengthening cooperative activities. A Memorandum of Understanding was signed for a US dollar 300 million joint venture fertilizer project in the Qeshm Island in Iran and a US dollar 45 million project was awarded to Hindustan Machine Tools for supply of equipments and auxiliary vehicle for the Tehran Metro Workshop. IRCON secured a US dollar 25 million project for the execution of Ahwaz-Bandar-e-Imam Signalling Project.

India maintained satisfactory contacts with Algeria. An Indian Railway delegation visited Algiers in July-August 1994 for further cooperation in transport sector. Engineers India Ltd signed a fresh contract with Alteria's state-owned oil and gas company (SONATRACH) worth US dollar five million for providir.g consultancy services.

The Secretary-General of the Ministry of Foreign Affairs of Djibouti visited India in June 1994 for bilateral talks. It was decided to set up a Joint Committee at Secretary level. India supplied 23 tonnes of milk powder worth Rs. 10 lakh in September 1994 and has also agreed to offer technical assistance under ITEC and slots under the General Cultural Schlorarship Scheme (GCSS) to students from Djibouti wishing to pursue studies in India.

India and Egypt made renewed efforts to impart greater dynamism to the existing friendly and cordial relations which were reflected in the close interaction with various interantional fora. A 9-member Egyptian Parliamentary delegation led by Speaker of the People's Assembly of Egypt visited India in May 1994 and Egyptian Minster of State for Population and Family Welfare visited in January 1995. Foreign Secretary visited Egypt in August 1994 for mutual consultations on matters of common interest and concen. An Indian delegation led by the Health and Family Welfare Minister participated in the UN-sponsored International Conference on Population and Development (ICPD) held in Cairo in September 1994. Two-way trade with Egypt improved considerably during the year. Seventeen Indian companies and an official delegation led by Telecommunication Miniter participated in th Africa Telecom Exhibition held in Cairo in April 1994.

The year witnessed a number of high level exchanges between India and Israel. There Memoranda of Understanding each were signed between Indian and Israeli educational institutions during the visit of the Indian Minister of Human Resource Development and between the Indian enterprises and the Israeli companies during the visit of Chief Minister of Haryana. Some of the agreements signed during visits by Israeli delegations are an Air Transport Agreement signed during the visit of the Israeli Deputy Foreign Minister, a Memorandum of Understanding in telecommunications during the visit of Minister of Science, Arts and Communications and a Trade Agreement signed during the visit of Trade and Industry Minister. The year witnessed a quantum jump in the bilateral trade between Israel and India. Progress was achieved in cooperation in bio-technology, agriculture, dairy industry, drip irrigation and solar energy.

Relations with Jordan continued to remain friendly and were marked by high level contacts. India welcomed the Jordan-Israel agreement signed at Wadi Araba on 26 October 1994 and an Indian delegation led by Shri Salman Khurshid, Minister of State for External Affairs was present during the signing ceremony. Minister of Agriculture visited Jordan in June 1994 and Foreign Secretary held bilateral discussions on 23 August 1994 with Secretary General of the Jordanian Ministry of Foreign Affiars.

Following the end to the civil war in Lebanon there has been widening of bilateral contacts. With the visits of Minister of Agriculture in June and Foreign Secretary in August 1994 to Lebanon for bilateral discussions, commercial and cultural contacts with Lebanon have been resumed.

India's relations with Morocco were marked by cordiality, cooperation and understanding. The Indian delegation led by Sh. R.L. Bhatia, Minister of State for External Affairs participated in the first Middle East/ North Africa Economic Summit held in Casablanca in October 1994.

India's relations with the PLO continue to be marked by cordiality, close understanding and a complementarity of views. India has been a consistent supporter for the legitimate aspirations of the Palestinian people and welcomed the Israel-PLO agreement signed in Cairo on 4 May 1994, which set up the Palestinian National Authority (PNA) and put into process the withdrawal of Israeli tropps from Gaza and Jericho. An Indian delegation led by the Minister of State for External Affairs, Shri R.L. Bhatia was present during the signing ceremony. India has been a strong supporter of and has enthusiastically participated in the Middle East Peace Process (MEPP) meetings. India has regularly contributed to the United Nations Relief and Works Agency (UNRWA) budget and has also offered to train 15 para-medical staff from Gaza and Jericho. India has proposed to send a team to conduct feasibility studies for setting up a Hi-Tech Centre on Computers and Electronics that will train Palestinian youth and help address the unemployment problem of Gaza and Jericho and has also decided to send 100 metric tonnes of tea to the region.

India sent medicines and seeds worth Rs. 10 lakh to Somalia. Both India and Sudan have sought to widen the scope of their bilateral cooperation and re-establish their multi-dimensional links. First Under Secretary of the Sudanese Ministry of Foreign Affairs visited India in April 1994 to discuss various issues of mutual concern. It was also decided to increase the share of Sudan in the ITEC programme. An Agreement to set up a Joint Committee at the Secretary-level was signed during the visit of Secretary (East) to Sudan January 1995.

Bilateral relations with Syria continued to get warmer. The Minister of Agriculture visited Syria in June 1994. A Programme of Cooperation in the field of agriculture and allied sectors was signed between the two sides. Foreign Secretary visited Syria in August 1994.

The 7th session of the Indo-Tunisian Joint Commission took place in New Delhi in September 1994. A Commercial Agreement was signed between the two sides and have exchanged draft treaties on extradition. India maintained traditionally close relations with the League of Arab States and values the efforts made by the League to develop and strengthen friendship between India and the Arab countries.

India made sincere attempts to persuade the Organisation of Islamic Conference to adopt objective and unbiased views on India-specific issues. The Seventh Extra Ordinary Islamic Foreign Ministers Conference held in Islamabad in September passed a resolution for establishing an OIC Contact Group on Kashmir at the UN. India regretted the resolution. Subsequent attempts by the OIC Contact Group to table an India-specific draft resolution in the First Committee of the UNGA had to be given up due to lack of support from the member countries themselves following India's extensive demarches to the concerned countries to explain her position in this regard. While the Seventh Islamic Summit held in Casablanca (Morocco) in December 1994 passed the customary resolution on Jammu and Kashmir dispute, there was a pronounced shift away at the Summit from the bilateral disputes.

International Relations and Regional Co-operation

ertain developments have consolidated themselves and others are becoming visible in the international system following the end of the Cold War. Considered from the perspectives of politics, economics and strategy the common threat running throuhg them is greater centralisation and decentralisation simultaneously in the international polity. The parallel with the centrifugal forces, which distinguished South Asian polity in the historical frame work, is too obvious to be missed. But the difference between the processes familiar to South Asia and what is happening in the world today is that these dialiectically opposed forces are working conjointly in the international system.

The disintegration of the Soviet Union has unleashed forces of heightening divergence: growing ethno-political differences in the former Republics presage the emergence of further political entities. For that matter what is happening in the former Yugosalavia could also inspire similar developments in Eurasia. A fillip has been provided to subnational, centrifugal forces within nations that could disrupt national entities, although they could be represented as anti-status quo forces that challenge the existing power hierarchies and obtaining political systems. This, too, would strengthen beliefs that centrifugal developments are on the ascendancy in the international system.

However, strong intimations are also present favouring the construction of larger politico-economic structures to derive the advantages and benefit from greater unity in cooperative action. The new role assumed by the United Nations is a pointer in this direction. The Commonwealth of Independent States is an example of the efforts to retrieve as much as possible from the debris of past politics and economics. Attempts to construct similar structures in East Asia and to invigorate existing multinational arrangements, especially in the spheres of trade and economic cooperation, emphasize the reality that forces encouraging the convergence of polities are simultaneously obtaining in the world.

Similar divergent and convergent movements are taking shape in the area of international security. Although the Warsaw Pact has broken up, desperate attempts are afoot to keep NATO alive, despite the

Soviet threat having disappeared. Consequently, operational tasks are being discovered for NATO outside its traditional areas of operations which, incidentally, include Asia and Africa. Developments within Russia and Ukraine/C.I.S. are also believed to require the Western Alliance's continuance. Areas of tension and instability also continue in existence across Eurasia, ranging from the Korean peninsula to Bosnia and Georgia, that could presage external intervention. But there are signs of peace and stability descending upon the war-torn Middle East with the recent agreement signed by the bitterly hostile leaders of Israel and the P.L.O. And, of the end of apartheid coming near with the evolution of democratic processes in that country based on universal franchise.

The area of proliferation of weapons of mass destruction is similarly witnessing strong efforts by the nuclear weapons powers and their allies to constrain the emergence of further nations that would either acquire nuclear weapons or ballistic missiles. These efforst would gain further urgency and momentum as the NPT Review Conference, scheduled for mid-1995, draws nearer. On the other hand, several international developments have occurred as in the former Soviet Republics, North Korea and South Africa that suggest the likelihood of a more largely proliferated world coming into being.

Turning to South Asia's immediate neighbourhood, ASEAN has reached a stature that commends emulation by SAARC. Indeed, the growth of greater economic/ political linkages between the countries of East Asia and South-east Asia might consign South Asia to the backwaters of the global economy. NAFTA and EEC, despite recurrent problems, are on the way to consolidating their likages, that could have the practical effect of shutting out the developing countries, or in allowing them some limited access for specific purposes, but with non-economic conditionalities attached. This is becoming increasingly apparent in the sphere of technology transfers, especially high technologies, that are being denied on the grounds that they could serve imaginatively presumed non-civil purposes.

South Asia must seek its destiny in this complex international milieu. The choices before it are stark and clearly evident, it could proceed by wise diplomacy and sincere efforts to sink differences and mutual suspicions and increase trade, economic, cultural, social and other ties to recreate the sense of kinship that has always distinguished the South Asia clan. Or, it could dissipate its energies in sterile controversies and disputes, leading to the need for maintaining costly military machines with their significantly high opportunity costs.

Looking ahead

The fifth decade of Independence has triggered investment interest in India as never before. Policymakers should now bring in a lot more clarity on their objectives.

The rules of international trade have changed. Witrh trade barriers getting dismantled by the day, there is need to infuse a very high degree of competitiveness. A major development is the evolution of regional trade groupings like the European Community (EC), the North American Free Trade Association (NAFTA), ASEAN, APEC etc.

Though the south Asian countries have formed the SAARC, progress achieved in free trade among these has been slow. Apart from mere trade flows, potential benefits in terms of the phasing out of poliltical animosities and more cohesive regional developments are immense.... The EC experience proves this. Over the last 50 years Britain, France and Germany, who have been bitter adversaries for centuries, have been bonded together on the strength of mutuality of economic interests. The SAARC union could grow to include China, the Central Asian Republics and the Indian Ocean rim countries, including South Africa, and forge close links with ASEAN and APEC in course of time. The comparable levels of economic development of most of the countries in this region would help in co-ordinated growth.

There is a huge market for such equiptment: there are capabilities in these countries to produce entire range of such equipment–generators, turbines, boilers, transformers, switchgears, motors et al.

The Korean automobile manufacturers—Daewoo Motors and Hyundai—indicate plants for developing India as a major centre for their global operations. Like we did in regard to Maruti, in the assimilation of mass production technology, India should attempt absorption of the high productivity levels of the Koreans, Americans and others; combine this with the strength of the massive availability of skilled manpower to win global markets.

United nations and international organisations

The United Nations (UN) is presently in the process of restructuring and reforming both in terms of institutions and concepts. India's efforts during 1994-95 were directed at influencing these changes in accordance with her world view and her perceptions of the role of the UN. India put forward concrete and forceful proposals at the Economic and Social coucil (ECOSOC), World Hearings on Development and at the General Assembly. The revised Agenda for Development represents a success of the Indian diplomacy.

India constituted a National Committee for Commemoration of the Fiftieth Anniversary of the UN and undertook a substantive year-long programme to mark the event. The celebration was inaugurated on 30 October 1994 by Prime Minister's address to the nation and a cultural programme, couped with a photographic exhibition.

During his visit to India in September 1994, the UN Secretary General, Boutros-Boutros Ghali expressed his gratitude for India's contribution to the UN Peace-Keeping activities. The President of the 48th Session of the General Assembly also visited India.

India continued to play a leading role in UN Peace-Keeping activities. Indian battalion to UN Operation in Mozambique (ONUMOZ) has returned home. India's 5,000 strong contingent to UN Operation in Somalia (UNOSOM II) whose commendable performance was acknowledged by the UN, the various factions in Somalia, the NGOs working for humanitarian relief, and the people of Somalia, returned home after their successful mission. India has provided a battalion to the UN Assistance Mission in Rwanda (UNAMIR) and has also agreed to contribute a brigade group to UN Standby forces, and to provide 100 doctors, engineers and trainers to UN Mission in Haiti (UNMIH), Phase II, in addition to a company of paramilitary forces.

At the 49th session of th UNGA, Commerce Minister stated that India deserve to be a permanent member of the Security Council and also announced her candidature to the non-permanent seat in the Security Council for the year 1996-97.

Pakistan move for an increase in the strength of UNMOGIP observers on both sides of the Line of Control has not found support in the Security Council. The UN Secretary General stressed his willingness to exert every possible effort to facilitate a search for a solution to the outstanding problems between India and Pakistan. India has made it very clear that she remains committed to the Shimla Agreement, which calls for resolution of all outstanding issues bilaterally. Pakistan tried to table a resolution against India in the First Committee of the UNGA through an OIC Contact Group, however prompt and effective counter-measures initiated by India forced Pakistan to abandon the move.

India had played a major role in the negotiations leading to the agreement related to implementation of Part XI of the UN Convention of the Law of the Sea concerning deep sea-bed mining and exploration, which was adopted unanimously by the resumed 48th session of the UNGA in June 1994.

In keeping with her long-standing approach to nuclear disarmament as the first step towards general and complete disarmament, India was actively associated with global measures for the elimination of nuclear weapons. In January 1994, an Adhoc Committee of the Conference on Disarmament on Nuclear Test Ban (NBT) with a full negotiating mandate to conclude a Comprehensive Test Ban Treaty (CTBT) was established. The Indian delegate is the Friend of Chair (FOC) on Seismic Methods under the Working Group on Verification. A draft 'rolling text' of the CTBT was finalised in September 1994. India tabled a resolution on the subject of a Convention on the Prohibition of the Use and Threat of Use of Nuclear Weapons which the First Committee of the UN adopted with 98 votes in favour. India also co-sponsored a new resolution calling for a step-by-step reduction of the nuclear weapons which was adopted by the First Committee with 91 votes in favour. India's proposal for the convening of a Fourth Special Session of the General Assembly devoted to Disarmament (SSOD-IV) taken up enthusiastically by NAM and presented as a NAM initiative at the last session of the UNGA. A consensus resolution agreeing to the convening of such a session of the UNGA. A consensus resolution agreeing to the convening of such a session in 1997 was adoped by the First Committee of the UNGA.

India was also actively involved in UN expert groups on the Register on Conventional Arms, the Inhumane Weapons Convention, and Verificaion in All Its Aspects. India continued her principled opposition to ad hoc export control regimes such as the Australia Group, Nuclear Suppliers Group (NSG) and the Missile Technology Control Regime (MTCR) in various international fora and called for their conversion into universal, transparent, non-discriminatory treaties which clearly distinguish between civilian and military applications. An MTCR Quad team consisting of representations of Switzerland, US, UK and Australia visited India on 30 August 1994 for official level discussions.

A Special Conference of the States Parties of the Biological Weapons Convention (BWC) was held at Geneva in September 1994 in which India participated actively as one of the Vice Presidents. An ad hoc group of experts was set up to consider verification measures for the BWC.

India continued bilateral dialogues on disarmament, non-proliferation and security-related issues with the USA, France and Germany. Bilateral initiatives resulted in (i) the issuance of a joint statement by Prime Minister Shri P.V. Narsimha Rao and President Clinton in May 1994 offering their strong support for efforts towards non-proliferation of weapons of mass destruction and their means of delivery and towards the progressive reduction with the goal of elimination of such weapons and (ii) a joint declaration issued by prime Minister Shri P.V. Narsimha Rao and President Yeltsin reiterating their commitment to all measures aimed at the complete and universal elimination of the weapons of mass destruction. India also utilised these dialogues to effectively project her position that her security concerns cannot be addressed in the narrow framework of India-Pakistan relations but as part of a global problem which would require a global solution.

Regarding human rights, India's consistent stand in the UN fora was that it should be pursued in the Vienna spirit of cooperation and consensus. During 1994-95, the National Human Rights Commission was established through an Act of the Parliament. A number of envoys visited Jammu and Kashmir which reflect India's policy of transparency in protection and promotion of human rights. During the 50th session of the Commission on Human Rights in Geneva in March 1994, a resolution on Human Rights and Terrorism was adopted by consensus. India participated as an observer in the 46th session of the UN Sub-Commission on Prevention of Discrimination and Protection of Minorities in August 1994. Pakistani moves to float a resolution were successfully thwarted, while the adoption at the 49th UNGA Declaration on Measures to Eliminate International Terrorism was an achievement of India's diplomacy in the United Nations. It called upon all States to take effective measures to prevent, combat and eliminate terrorism.

India continued to play an active role in the ECOSOC, the Governing Boards of the specialised agencies, various international meetings on the issue of promotion and protection of environment, and in the Second Committee of the United Nations.

The Second Session of the Commission on Sustainable Development (CSD), including the High Level Segment, held in May 1994 in New York was attended by the Minister of State for Environment and Forests. India was elected to the Bureau and became a

Vice Chairman, representing Asia. India was also elected as the Chairperson of the Working Group I of the CSD.

India signed the Convention to Combat Desertification with Special Reference to Africa which was finalised at the Fifth Meeting of the Inter-governmental negotiating Committe in Paris in 1994.

In the second session of the Inter-governmental Committee on Convention on Bio-Diversity held in Nairobi in June 1994, India was able to seek endorsement from the G-77 and effectively project her views on the issue of conclusion of a Protocol on Bio-Safety, Farmers' Rights and *ex-situ* collections, collections of CGIAR system, criteria for selection of the Secretariat.

As a recognition of the prominent role played by India, the Indian member was unanimously elected as the first Chairman of the GEF Executive Council. India is a donor and recipient nation and has contributed SDR six million (US dollar 8.5 million approximately) to the total GEF corpus of US dollar two billion. India hosted the 50th session of the ESCAP in New Delhi in April 1994, and also continued to take an active part in various activities for the Asia and Pacific region organised by ESCAP.

At the third International Conference on Population and Development held in Cairo in September 1994, India pointed out that the problem of demographic growth could only be addressed through integrated solutions, encompassing health, family welfare, education, women empowerment, employment and eradication of poverty. India participated actively in the discussions in the second and the third sessions of the PREPCOM for the World Summit for Social Development held in New York in August September 1994 and in January 1995.

India was a member of the Ad hoc Group

established to investigate fraud within the UN system, and also remained a member of the Board of Auditors of the UN and voiced concern over the mounting expenditure on peace-keeping operations and the delayed or non-payment of assessments by the member States. It was elected/nominated to the Commission on Transnational Corporations; the Inter-governmental Working Group of Experts on International Standards of Accounting and Reporting; the Committee on Non-Government Organisations; the Executive Board of UNICEF; the Committee for UN Population Award; the UN Administrative Tribunal; the Commission on Human Rights of ECOSOC; the Postal Operations Council and Consultative Council for Postal Studies of the Universal Postal Union; the Administrative Council of the International Telecommunications Union; the Human Rights Committee of the International Covenant of Civil and Political Rights (ICCPR); and the Economic and Social Council (ECOSOC). India was also elected as the Vice Presidents of the 49th Session of the UN General Assembly and the Commission on Sustainable Development and as the Chairman of several of the international meetings held in the region under ESCAP.

India participated actively in the NAM meetings and took active interest in the work of the Coordinating Bureau of the Movement in New York. The Fifth Conference of the Labour Ministers of Non-Aligned and other Developing Countries inaugurated by the Prime Minister on 19 January 1995, adopted the Delhi Declaration and a Plan of Action.

India continued to participate actively in meetings of the Commonwealth's over-arching governance mechanisms. The Commonwealth Secretary General who officially visited India in December 1994 paid tribute to India's contribution to the concept of a modern Commonwealth which had allowed it to outgrow an

Anglo-centric past and expressed the hope that the Commonwealth philosophy of mutual help and Jawarhar Lal Nehru's legacy of the 'healing touch' would held the Commonwealth to serve members better.

India participated in the 46th Session of the International Law Commission (ILC) which was held at Geneva in July 1994 and the 27th session of the United Nations Commission on International Trade Law (UNCITRAL) held at New York. India also actively parcipated in the deliberations of the Sixth (Legal) Committee at the 49th Session of the UNGA, the annual session of the Legal Sub-Committee of the UN committee on Peaceful Uses of Outer Space at Vienna in March/ April 1994 and the meeting of legal experts of States signatory to the Antartica Treaty, held at The Hague in November 1994. India became a party to several multilateral Conventions.

International economic environment

1. With the progress of economic reforms in many countries of the world and deregulation of financial markets, the importance of private capital flows into Asia has increased from US $ 76.8 billion in 1994 to US $ 98.0 billion in 1995, while net official flows increased marginally from US $ 5.6 billion to US $6.4 billlion during the same period. Similarly, while there were considerable official flows to Mexico and the transition countries in 1995 in support of their comprehensive adjustment programmes, net private capital flows to the developing countries increased from US $ 140.4 billion in 1994 to US $ 166.6 billion in 1995. India has has modest, but increasing, success in attracting a growing part of these private capital flows. Furthermore, much of these private capital inflows into India has been of the non-debt creating variety, and helped to boost the balance of

payments as well as the availability of investible resources in the economy.

2. The international financial community is appreciative of India's economic performance in the last years, but concerns continue to be expressed about the high fiscal deficit, the slowing down of structural reforms, continued restrictions on consumer goods imports, and tariff levels considerably higher than in other countries. Also, references are often made to India's move towards capital account convertibility (with some observers advocating a cautions approach), high level of subsidies, inadequate disinvestment in the public sector, need for further relaxation of rules to attract foreign investment and the continued high stake of the government in the public sector banks. On the whole, the international community is very positive about India's effort to achieve a high rate of growth.

3. Participants in the India Development Forum (IDF) meeting in September 1996 acknowledged the strong performance of the Indian economy and appreciated the new Government's declaration to continue reform measures to strengthen the social programmes as set out in the Common Minimum Programme (CMP). Various delgates stressed the importance of (i) fiscal consolidation, (ii) sustaining programmes in the social sectors, (iii) infrastructrue, (iv) provety eradication, (v) reforms in agriculture, public sector, and financial sector, and (vi) strengthening of legislation against child labour. In support of India's economic development, the donor countries pledged official assistance in 1996-97 of US $ 6.7 billion. Inclusion of US $ 400 million in long-term finance, promised on a bilateral basis at market rates, will raise this total to above US $ 7 billion.

About 33 per cent of the total could be in the form of grants and interest-free loans.

4. With effect from January 1, 1997, India subscribed to the Special Data Dissemination Standards (SDDS) of the International Monetary Fund (IMF). by subscribing to the SDDS, India ha committed itself to streamilining the tatistical system of the country to produce most of the data categories with a much shorter time lag, improved quality and coverage by December 31, 1988.

Foreign economic relations

Government of India continued to give special and focussed attention to economic diplomacy at the bilateral, regional and multilateral levels. Government's efforts is to expand existing opportunities and create new ones for trade, investment and technological cooperation with the industrialised, newly industrialising and developing countries.

India's engagement in economic cooperation among a trans-regional group of developing countries in Asia, Latin America and Africa assumed special significance. The 4th Summit of the G-15 was held in New Delhi from 28 to 30 March 1994. It was decided to broaden the scope of intra G-15 cooperation through the establishment of a Committee of Trade, Investment and Technology to work towards evolution of trans-regional arangements for liberalisation, facilitation and promotion of trade, investment and technology transfer. The Summit decided to harness the information and communication revolution to promote better understanding and knowledge of capabilities, potential and experiences of G-15 countries among each other and extend full support through appropriate projects for expanding cooperation in setting up of small scale industreis.

At the 30th Anniversary commemoration meeting of the Group of 77 held in New York in July 1994, India reaffirmed the historical validity of the concept, purpose and endeavours of the Group of 77. By inserting a development dimension and consensus in international institutions and policies, the G-77 had acted as a development conscience of the world and recorded some gains in this respect.

Progress has been made in establishment on an ASEAN-India Trade and Investment Information and Promotion Centre, collaboration and joint ventures in India, ASEAN and third countries; cooperation in tourist destination, development and exchange of information and technology.

In July 1994 India gave a detailed presentation to OECD on economic reforms inititated by India, which was followed by a visit by the President of the OECD Development Centre to India. A break-through in closer association with the OECD was achieved in December 1994 when the OECD Council approved inclussion of India along with Indonesia and China in their OECD Policy Dialogue framework with Dynamic New Major Economies (DNMEs). India continued to further fine tune, adapt and expand her ECDC and TCDC programmes under the ITEC programme and the SCAAP for the benefit of developing countries mainly in Africa, Latin America, Caribbean and South East Asia. During 1994-95, 875 slots have been allocated for training of foreign nominees in Indian civilian institutions and 65 regular courses are being held in 30 prominent institutions in banking, small scale industries, finance, tool research, etc. India also offered military training to nominees from friendly foreign countreis.

Under the ITEC programme, projects are executed in partner countries, among other things, such projects serve as demonstration models highlighting India's technology and potential in specific areas. Under execution are Vocational Training Centres in Vietnam and Mongolia, Solar Photovoltaic Plants in Oman and Cuba, a Remote Sensing Centre in Mauritius and a Mobile Eye Clinic in Ghana. Execution of feasibility studies/extension of consultancy services in partner countries are also undertaken under ITEC.

The SCAAP programme is aimed at providing technical assistance by India to 15 African counries which are ex-colonies of UK. In 1994-95, a total of 475 slots were allocated to nominees from Ghana, Nigeria, Mauritius, Tanzania and Zambia. A new dimension was attempted to be given to Indian's policy of South-South Cooperation through the Special volunteers Programme (SVP). The SVP envisages the sending of special volunteers to developing countries in Africa and Asia to assist them in their development programmes. During 1994-95, disaster relief assistance has been/is being extended to Armenia, Tanzania, Mozambique, Afghanistan, Uzbekistan, Rawanda, Somalia, Madagascar, Djibouti, Mauritius, etc. Such humanitarian gestures strike a positive chord amongst the people of these countries and create goodwill for India.

Trade and investment promotion

One of the most important forces current developments today is the emergence of a truly global economy. India's economic reforms programme reflects her determination to build an economy that is internationally competitive and integrated into the global economy.

Investment promotion seminars have been organised in Japan, Germany, singapore, Thailand, Australia,l Italy and USA, wide publicity was given to international fairs organised in India like IITF'94, International Seminar on Mineral and Mineral-based industries in ESCAP Region'94, MANTECH'95, IETF'95, AGROEXPO'95, Gifts and Handicrafts Fair'95 and 22nd World Marketing and Management congress'95. Special efforts were made to reach out to business journalists in foreign countries by arranging their visits to India in order to enable them to see first hand the changes in the business environment. Prime Minister's visits to the UK, Russia, USA, Vietnam and Singapore, as well as visits by Ministers and prominent economic personalities were utilised to highlight the opportunities for economic collaborations and business tie-ups with India. In the course of the Prime Minister's visit to Singapore in September 1994, 12 agreements were signed between Indian and Singaporean companies in diverse fields.

Various investment promotion seminars were also organised in India.Prominenet among these were INVESTMART organised in April 1994 by Ministry of Industry in collaboration with UNIDO. The entire forum was focussed on promoting 250 specific projects identified in specific sectors by Ministry of Industry. France, Italy, UK, USA and Singapore participated. About 70 Letters of Intent for identified projects were signed between Indian entrepreneurs and foreign collaborators.

Trade scenario in Post-Independence era

By virtue of the radical shift from a highly-regulated to an outward-oriented economy, India has generated immense interest abroad, but it has a long way to go before emerging as a strong global player, opines the author.

India's development strategy launched in the 1950s, soon after Independence, aimed mainly at strengthening the industrial base of the country, especially in basic goods and heavy machine-building, and adopted the import-substituation model to achieve self-reliance.

Rxports were not viewed as an integral part of overall economic development, and such imports as became unavoidable were financed by drawing down foreign exchange reserves that had accrued to India at the time of Independence, in the form of sterling balances held in its favour for goods and services provided by this country during the Second World War.

Export pessimism dominated the mood of the early planners as it was rightly assumed then that until India's manufactures began to be diversified, there was little possibility of exporting manufactures while primary products and traditional manufactured goods faced poor demand prospects in the world market. It was during the later half of the fifties, when the Second Five Year Plan was under way with its emphasis on heavy industry, largely in the public sector, that it began to be realised that India needed to export to be able to finance at least part of the maintenance and developmental imports.

The foreign exchange crisis that was looming by mid-1957 reinforced the importance of export growth as part of planned development. *The pessimistic view about the potential for export earnings gave way to a more positive approach in the Third Plan (1961-66) with the introduction of export promotion measures without deflecting from the thrust of import subsitution and industrialisation.* It was clear by mid-estimated the import content of the inward-looking path of development opted by India. Pressures on balance of pyaments had already brought into existence the Aid-India-Consortium comprising the World Bank and developed countries interested in providing assistance to India. Renewed emphasis on exports was laid in the Fourth Plan (1969-74) which envisaged porogressive elimination of dependence on foreign aid while the Fifth Plan (1974-79) identified certain sectors such as engineering goods, garments, leather manufacture and marine products for achieving increases in exports.

Thus, as agianst virtual stagnation in the 1950s, export performance improved to an average growth of 3 to 4 per cent in the 1960s, and was more impressive in 1970s with an average growth of 6.3 per cent in volume and 15.9 per cent in value terms.

But in the three decades, India's share in world exports had declined throughout from about 2 per cent in 1950 to 0.65 per cent in 1970 and dropped further to 0.42 per cent in 1980. This was the period when there was impressive grow thin world trade and the opportunities were seize by many smaller Asian developing countries as well as the industrialising economies in Latin America to great advantage.

Paradoxically, even as india's export growth was being maintained or marginaly improved upon, her share of world exports was declining. Over the three decades ending the Seventies, the share of exports in Gross Domestic Product (GDP) ranged from 4 to 6 per cent. *In a continental economy of India's size, the role of external sector in the development process was under-played so much that it took a successions of droughts, oil price shocks and balance of payments difficulties in the first two and a half decades of planning before the country could begin to see import substitution and export promotion as two sides of the same coin.* But heavy reliance on quantitative restrictions on trade through import and export controls and detailed industrial licensing kept India a closed economy.

3

Industrial Policy and Trade Policy of the Government of India

India Investment Centre

Industrial policy

Over the years the Government of India has been adopting various measures for the liberalisation of the Industrial Policy, for streamling the licensing and foreign collaboration procedures, for reducing the number of agencies which the prospective investors have to approach to get the necessary approvals, etc., with the objective of attracting more investment and technology transfer. On the 24th July, 1991 the Government tabled before Parliament the Statement on Industrial Policy, 1991, which was followed by the issuance of a Notification by the Department of the Industrial Development to implement the Policy Statement and a series of Press Notes to set out the changes in the existing system and procedure for obtaining industrial licenses and approval of proposals for foreign and for foreign testing of indigenous raw materials and products and indigenously developed technlogies.

Industrial licensing policy

The new Industrial Licensing Policy of the Government of India has exempted form the requirement of obtaining industrial licence all industries, except those reserved for the Public Sector (Schedule I to the the Notification), those in respect of which Idustrial Licensing is compulsory (Schedule II to the Notification) and those relating to the items reserved for exclusive manufacture in the small scale sector (Schedule III to the Notification).

The exemption from Industrial licensing is also subject to:

— The proposed project (except in the case of a project relating to electronics, computer software, printing industry, industry located within an area designated as 'industrial area' by a State Government before the 25th July, 1991 or the small scale or the ancillary sector) being not located with 25 kilo meters form the periphery of the standard urban area limits of a city having a population of more than one million according to the 1991 census; and

— Of the Central and the State environmental laws and regulations including local zoning and land use laws and regulations.

Units qualifying for exemption from industrial licensing in accordance with the foregoing conditions are required only to file a Memorandum in the prescribed form, before establishement of the project, with the Department of Industrial Development (Secretariat for Industrial Approvals) together with a crossed demand draft for rupees one thousand in favour of the Pay and Account Officer, Department of Industrial Development and another Memorandum in the prescribed form at the time of commencement of commercial production.

Small scale and ancillary units are required, as before, to be registered with the Director of Industries of the concerned State. Manufacturing units with an investment in plant and machinery up to Rs. 60 lakhs, ancillary units with an investment in plant and machinery up to Rs. 75 lakhs and units which are willing to undertake an export obligation to the extend of 30 per cent of their annual production by the third year with an investment up to Rs. 75 lakhs are eligible for small scale registration.

Foreign investment policy

The new industrial policy of the Government of India has announced major liberalisation for attracting foreign investment in respect of a list of high priority industries (Annexure III to the Statement of Industrial Policy, 1991). Foreign equity investment up to 51 per cent will be allowed subject only to the condition that:

— The requirement of imported capital goods should be covered by the foreign equity;

— Remittance of dividends should be covered by earnings of the company from export of items in Annexure III to the Statement of Industrial Policy, 1991. The amount of dividend payment may be converted by export earnings of such items recorded in Years prior to the payment of dividend or in the year of payment of dividend. This will be monitored by the Reserve Bank of India. However, such balancing will not be required beyond a period of seven years from commencement of production.

In all such cases the Reserve Bank of India has been authorised to issue automatic approvals of foreign investment and also grant exemption from the operation of the relevant sections of the Foreign Exchange Regulations Act, 1973.

Ushering in an era of scripless trading

The Primary issuance of securities has a long history in India. The Indian bond market, measured by the estimated value of bonds outstanding, is next only to the Japanese and the Korean bond market in Asia. By January 31, 1995, the outstanding value of the Indian securities market was estimated to have reached Rs.3000 billion, almost 3.5 times its size in 1986. The size is deceptive as, despite attractive yields, secondary market trading has remained poor with virtually no quotation even in respect of listed securities. The estimated outstanding amount accounts for about 42% of GDP, as at the end of January 1995. Partial deregulation of interest rates in the early nineties and increasing emphasis on monetary policy in stabilization are the first major steps towards the emergence of an active debt market, with government securities spearheading the process. With the issuance of government securities at market determined coupon rates and the use of innnovative products, it has become possible, for the first time, for other issuers to offer debt products priced off the yield on government securities.

The process of financial sector reforms initiated in 1991, is far from complete. The Growth of the Indian Capital Market since Independence has been phenomenal. The number of stock exchanges increased from 7 in 1947 to 23 in 1994. Likewise the number of listed companies on stock exchanges grew from 1125 in 1946 to 7811 at the end of 994. Similarly, the quantum of listed capital registered a growth of about 565 times from Rs.270 crore in 1946 to Rs.152,322 crore at the end of March, 1994.

The basic objective of financial sector reforms is to promote a diversified, efficient and competitive financial system by a policy shift from detailed regulation and controls to one based on market forces. Alongwith dismantling administrative regulation, the goal is establishment of a system of prudential regulation, supported by a mechanism for reporting, monitoring and supervision of the compliance.

Another major plan of reform is injection of new competition into a hitherto virtually government owned financial system. For the first time in many years, six new banking licences have been granted to the private sector all of which have been implemented. The new banks are permitted to have financial joint ventures with fgoreign baks, particularly for accessing modern systems and technology. There has been a mushrooming of Non-Banming Finance Companies (NBFCs), some of whom have already built up a large net-work. Several well known investment banks have established a presence in India. Since April 1993, nearly 300 Foreign Institutional Inestors (FIIs) have been registered with the regulatory authority and quite a few are active investors in the domestic capital market which has been opened up to foreign portfolio investment in a limited way. Several new mutual funds have been set up by the private sector including some by global fund managers. The most spectacular growth has been registered when we compare the share of market capitalization to gross domestic products (GDP) which was 12.9% in 1946, while in 1991-92 it was 57.2% and further increased to 68.8% during 1993-984.

Trade policy

Side by side with the announcement of New Industrial Policy for Promoting Small Tiny and Village Enterprises, the Government have also announced major reforms in the Trade Policy. The main objective of the trade policy have been to progressively reduce the system of administrative controls and lilcences and to link import except in the case of essential items. The major reforms in the Trade Policy are given below:

Introduction of eximscrip system

Exports were in the past allowed replenishment to provide for essential inputs required for the manufacture of products exported. To allow flexibility to enable diversification of export products and also as an incentive for exports, the REP licenses so issued, were allowed to be freely sold. The entitlement for REP licenses also varied from item to item. In view of the flexibility of the REP Licenses Government realise that to treat it as licence is an misnomer, under the new policy the REP licences have been replaced by a new instrument named 'Eximscrips'. Eximscrips will be issued on the basis of FOB value of exports or Net FOreign Exchange (NFE) earnings from exports as indicated below. The main features of the new systems are:

(i) The basic rate at which Eximscripts will be issued against exports will be 30% of FOB value. Exports to hard currency areas will be eligible for Eximscrips valid for hard currency imports while exports to rupee payment areas will be issued Eximscrips valid for imports from these areas only. However, as a measure of transition, exports to rupee payment areas may continue to avail of REP licences valid for hard currency imports at the rate prevailing prior to 4th July, 1991. This transition facility will be available only for exports effected upto 31st December 1991.

(ii) Products such as gems and jewellery, handcrafts, newspapers, journals and periodicals and cinematographic films, which enjoyed higher rated of REP will receive Eximscrips at the same rates as before.

(iii) The Basis rate of 30% is inadequate for exports of certain products such as value-added agricultural projects, electronics, bulk drugs and marine products, formulations and certain categories of advanced engineering goods. These products will be eligible for an additional Eximscrips entitlement of 10 percentage points, taking the total Eximscrips rate to 40% of FOB value.

For exports made on the basis of duty free imports obtained against Advance Licences, Eximscrips will be available at the general rate of 30% but this will be applied to the net foreign exchange earnings. On the same principle. Eximscrips at 30% of NFE will also be available for all EOU and EPZ units.

(iv) The 30% of NFE rate of Eximscrips is also applicable to service exports, including software exports which is a thrust area. The definition of services covered under this category is being ratinallized and extended to include other services such as services of architects, textile designers, artists, management consultants, lawyers etc. The benefit will be available to services exported by resident Indians for which remittances are made to India. The details are being notified separately.

Eximscrips issued to exporters will be tradeable and can be used to import any item in the limited permissible list (Appendix-3), the non-sensitive canalised list (Appendix-5A) and for all OGL, items for actual users (Appendix-6, List 8, Part I and List 10). Eximscrips earned by exporters on their own exports can also be used to import non-OGL capital goods other than those on the restricted list (Appendix-1A). All REP licences issued against exports prior to 4th July, 1991 will continue to be valid for the life of the licence and will have the same import entitlement as the new Eximscrips. Additional licences issued to export houses/trading houses, which were earlier valid for a more limited range of imports, will also be valid for the same range of imports as Eximscrips.

With the introduction of Eximscrips, the system of issuing supplementary licences of raw material, components and spares listed in Appendix-3 will be discontinued except for small scale industries and for manufacturers of specified life saving drugs and equipment. In future, all import requirements of these items (with the exceptions indicated above) will be made through Eximscrips, Similarly items in Appoendix-4 and Appendix-9, which were earlier importable against supplementary licences, will henceforth be importable only against Eximscrips. Import of items appearing in Appendix-2 Part B (list of Restricted Items) and Appendix-8 (List of Scientific and Measuring Instruments Restricted for Import) of the Import-Export Policy 1990-93 will continue to require licences. Such licences as well as licences required for small scale industries and manufactures of life saving drugs/equipment will be called Special Licences as these will be limited and include special cases.

As a measure of import compression and to strengthen the linkage between import capability and exports, two further changes have been made. The category of unlisted OGL has been abolished and these items have been shifted to Appendix-3. They are now importable only against Eximscrips (except for SSI and manufacturers of life saving drugs and equipment). In the case of units subject to the Phased Manufacturing Programme (PMP), many of which benefit from concessional duty on their imports of OGL items, all such items will henceforth be importable only against Eximscrips.

Eximscrips will be issued only after export proceeds have been realised. The procedure for issue of Eximscrips has been streamlined and Government will ensure that Eximscrips are issued within 48 hours of the receipt of the application accompanied by single document, namely, the bank certificate for the realisation of export proceeds.

Advance licences

The system of advance licences is designed to provide exporters with duty free access to the inputs they need to produce competitively for world markets. This is an important instrument of trade policy especially in our situation where tariff levels are still high. The Government has taken the following steps to strengthen the system of Advance Licences as an instrument of export promotion:

(i) The procedures for considering Advance Licence applications have been simplified to ensure that advance licences will be issued within 15 days of application in all cases where input-output norms have been fixed. Where norms have not been fixed, the licence will be issued within 45 days.

(ii) The number of documents accompanying an Advance licence application has been reduced from 9 to 3 where norms are prescribed and to 4 where they are not prescribed.

(iii) Ar present norms have been prescribed for 540 items. This will be increased to over 1000 items by 31st October, 1991 and more items will be covered thereafter.

(iv) Substantial Manufacturing Activity as a necessary condition under the Advance Licence Scheme will no longer be applicable for exports to the general currency area. However, the value addition norms will remain in force. A large number of exporters will benefit under this scheme.

(v) A new Scheme of Transferable Advance Licence has been introduced for GCA exports in selected thrust areas, namely textiles, leather goods and engineering industries. Under this scheme exporters can undertake exports based on duty paid inputs obtained from the market and subsequently obtain advance licences for replenishment of these inputs by duty free imports. These advance licences will be freely transferable. The coverage of the scheme will be extended on merits.

(vi) Advance licence will specify values in free foreign exchange both for the purpose of import and export. The currencies in which such values are denominated will be limited to those notified for this purpose by the RBI.

(vii) The Existing procedure for obtaining Bank Guarantee (BG) and Legal Undertaking (LUT) from different categories of exporters in being streamlined and liberalised as follows:

(a) Export/Trading/Star Trading House and Public Sector Undertakings will have the facility of obtaining advance licence against LUT only without any monetary limit.

(b) All manufacturing units having an annual turnover of at least Rs. 5 crores (including both domestic and exports turnover) during the previous 3 year would also be able to avail of the LUT facility up to a value limit of 50% of their annual production.

(c) A new unit without any production or export performance to its credit would also be allowed LUT facility provided it is promoted by an existing company with an annual production of Rs. 5 crores for more than three years. In such a case, both the new company and the promoting company would have to provide LUT.

(d) Bank guarantee and/or LUT obligation will be concurrent to the fulfilment of export obligation.

(viii) Exporters would be allowed to dispose of the materials imported against advance licences by way of replenishment without seeking prior permission of the licensing authority in cases where no MODVAT facility has been availed of on the domestic material used in exports.

(ix) Adjustment needed on account of fluctuation of prices of imported individual items would be permitted within the overall CIF value of advance licence.

(x) The power of revalidation which presently vests in the Licencing Committee at the Headquarters has been delegated to the Licensing Authorities.

(xi) In case where applications for an advance licence are turned down, the exporter will be permitted to convert to the Duty Drawback regime by the Collectors of Customs so that shipments made in advance can be imported on payment of duty subsequent claims of duty drawback.

(xii) Exporters can obtain advance release orders for domestic supply against advance licences under which the domestic supplier gets the benefit of deemed exports. Henceforth, release orders will be issued across the counter without requiring the name of the domestic supplier, which could be given later.

The adoption of these procedures would reduce discretionary controls and delays and afford much greater freedom to exporters in procuring essential duty free raw materials to maintain their competitiveness in the would market thereby promoting exports from the country.

Export processing zones and 100% EOUs

The export Processing Zone scheme and the 100% EOU scheme were introduced to provide for duty-free enclaves, which would enable entrepreneurs to concentrate on production exclusively for export. However, with increasing liberalisation in the DTA, the duty advantages enjoyed by EPZs/EOUs have become less important. While the procedures of Customs Bonding are very onerous. The schemes have not therefore taken off as expected and they have also not attracted foreign investment aimed at tapping export markets to the extent that was expected. The working of these schemes has been reviewed and the following changes made:

(i) All EOUs/EPZ unit will be eligible for Eximscrips at the basic rate of 30% applied to net foreign exchange earning.

(ii) The duty applicable on DTA sales from EOUs/EPZ units is being reduced to 50% of the normal customs subject to the duty payable not being less than the excise duty on the same product. The extent of DTA sales allowed will be accordance with their entitlement. DTA sales will be permitted in the ratio of 25:75 in relation to export sales in case of units while use of indigenous raw material is more than 30% of production. In all other cases the ratio of permissible DTA sales to export sales will be 15:85. The procedures for clearing goods from the EOU/EPZ units for DTA sales are also being streamlined.

(iii) In order to encourage exporters to set up EOUs or EPX units the net foreign exchange earned by EOUs or EPZ units can be clubbed with the earnings of their parent/associated companies in the DTA for the purpose of according Export House. Trading House of Star Trading House status for the latter.

(iv) The IPRS scheme for supply of steel to exporters will also be extended to EOUs and EPZ units. The Development Commissioners are being empowered to issue "payment authorities" in lieu of JCCI & Es.

Under the New Industrial Policy, most industries do not require an industrial licence except for a defined list. With a view to bringing about comparable streamlining in the procedure for EOU/EPZ approvals, a systems of automatic approvals is being established for all proposals which fall within certain parameters. Capital goods imports will be allowed under the automatic approvals procedure if they are fully covered by foreign equity or if they do not exceed 50% of the value of plant and equipment subject to a ceiling of Rs 3 crores. All proposals within the automatic approval parameters will be cleared within two weeks. All other proposals will be submitted to the Board of Approvals for consideration and decisions including issue of licences will be taken within 45 days.

A large number of issues relating to the operation of EOUs/EPZ units required centralized clearance in the Ministries of Commerce and Industry. Powers are being delegated to the Development Commissioners so that these approvals can be given on a decentralised basis. The specific approval of the Development Commissioner would not be required in cases of broad banding by EPZ units, where value addition is being maintained. The unit concerned would need only to provide relevant information to the Development Commissioner.

The following specific concessions to EOUs/EPZ units have also been extended:

(i) Allowing wntry of imported raw material on "Provisional Assessment" basis, to expedite customs clearance.

(ii) Permitting units under the EPZ and EOU schemes to supply/transfer finished goods among themselves.

(iii) Replacement of multiple bond by a single bond, for obtaining import clearance.

(iv) Increasing the list of items under the "Special Imprest Licence Scheme" on selective basis.

(vi) Clarifying that containers stuffed in EPZ and EOUs are not to be reinspected at cther points, as long as seals are intact.

Government have also decided to allow private parties to establish bonded warehouses within EPZs for stocking and sale of duty free raw materials, components, consumables and spares to EPZ units and EOUs. This will cut down delay in obtaining supplies of duty free materials which are in constant and regular demand by exporters. The details of this scheme will be notified shortly.

Other steps announced in the new Trade Policy have been the simplification of procedures for import of capital goods, decanalisation of number of items which were previously canalised, permission to allow established exporters to open foreign currency accounts in approved banks, raise external credits, pay for export related imports from such accounts and credit export proceeds to such accounts, its decision to re-designate the office of the Chief Controller of Import and Exports as Directorate General of International Trade with the principal function being to promote of exports, and facilitation of imports to promote export trade.

Reduction in import licence

The policy changes now being implemented imply substantial reduction in the extent of licensing and in the number of types of licences. Supplementary licences for import of items in Appendixes-3 (except for SSI and manufacturers of life saving drugs and equipment), 4 and 9 of the Import-Export Policy 1990-93 have been abolished. Additional licences which were issued as an incentive to Export Houses and Trading Houses will stand abolished with effect from 1st April, 1992 and the incentive will take the form of an additional Eximscrip entitlement.

To achieve optimal import containment in the context of the present Balance of Payments situation, several steps have been taken. One of these is the shift of many items which are on OGL to the limited permissible list.

With these changes, the policy for import of raw materials components and other inputs needed for production has been simplified. Most raw materials and other inputs (except for those on the Restricted List) can be freely imported either against Eximscrips or on OGL. Some raw materials continue to be canalised but in more of these cases requirements beyond those provided by the canalising agencies can be met through Eximscrips.It is the policy of the Government to move to a situation where imports of essential raw materials and components needed for industrial production are regulated through appropriate tariffs. However, in view of the Balance of Payments position which necessitates continued import containment, this cannot be done immediately. Many items must therefore remain on the limited permissible list, with imports permitted only against Eximscrips.

The medium term objective of the Government is to progressively eliminate licensing and quantitative restrictions on capital goods and raw materials/ components so that all these items can be placed on OGL save for a small carefully defined negative list. This shift is proposed to be achieved over a 3 to 5 year period. The Government will appoint a High Level Committee to work out the modalities of achieving this transition keeping in mind the Balance of Payments position and the need to rationalise the reduce tariffs progressively to provide Indian Industry with an appropriate environment to develop international competitiveness.

International trade and India

1. The important place commanded by India in world trade in coffee, tea, leather and spices on a historical basis has continued in recent years as wll. In 1994, India accounted for 2.4 per cent, 13.6 per cent, 2.5 per cent and 9.1 per cent of world trade in coffee and coffee substitues, tea and mate, leather, and spices, respectively. Furthermore, there has been a significant progress in export diversification, and India has emerged as an important exporter of iron ore and concentrates, and pearis, precious and semi-precious stones. In 1994, India accounted for 6 per

cent or world exports of iron ore and concentrates and 10.9 per cent of world exports of pearls, precious and semi precious stones (Source: 1994 United Nations International Trade Statistics Year Book, 1995).

2. During 1950, India accounted for about 1.8 per cent (1.85 per cent of exports and 1.71 per cent of imports) of world trade. After gradually declining to 0.57 per cent by 1980, India's share improved marginally to 0.63 per cent by 1985. The reason for improvement in the share was that while world trade declined in the period 1980-85, India's trade continued to grow. However it came down again to 0.53 per cent by 1991. The first half of the nineties witnessed a sharp increase in India's exports and imports have grown in dollar terms annually by 12.4 per cent and 9.4 per cent, respectively. The corresponding growth rates of world trade was about 5.7 per cent. The secular decline in India's share in world trade has been arrested and reversed, and the years ahead are likely to see a continuation of this increasing trend.

3. The trade policy components of the reform process undertaken since July 1991 have been motivated by a full recognition of the important role that trade can play in promoting growth. The utilisation of the expanded scope for specialising in areas of comparative advantage is manifest in the improved growth performance of the economy. Furthermore, while exports have vigorously responded to the removal of the anti-export bias of a protectionist environment, domestic industry appears to have been stimulated by the expended availability of imported inputs and capital goods as well as the challenge of competing in the international market place. The positive response of Indian industry to

liberalisation is amply demonstrated by the capital goods sector. The tariff on capital goods was as high as 85 per cent in the pre-reforms period. This has been reduced to about 25 per cent covering about 80 per cent of capital goods in 1995-96. The capital goods industry which witnessed a negative growth of 12.8 per cent in 1991-92, registered an average growth of about 23 per cent during 1994-96.

Terms of trade

4. The terms of trade, which measure the terms of exchange between a unit of exports and a unit of imports, have been improving in the post-reform period. Two common ways of measuring the terms of trade are the net terms of trade (NTT) and the income terms of trade (ITT). A time series indicating all parameters of terms of trade (TOT) for India since 1969-70 with the base of 1978-79 = 100 Indicates that there have been wide fluctuations in the TOT. The NIT (1978-79=100), which is an index of export prices divided by an index of import prices, improved from 109.3 in 1990-91 to 152.4 in 1994-95. It is

5. it may be mentioned that India s purchasing power of exports as reflected thorough ITT has been improving continuously since 1985- 86. The value index of exports at 484 stands much higher than that of imports at 351 and hence, in terms of value, india has gained.But in terms of volume, the index of exports has been much less at 384 in comparison to that of imports at 515. This means that the volume of imports is increassing faster, though India is getting a better price for her exports.

---

6. Compared to the experience of other developing countries, the improvement in the terms of trade for India has been very impressive. The NTT (1990=100),

as presented in the UN's International trade Statistics Year Book, 1995, is reproduced below:

Economies	1980	1985	1990	1991	1992	1993	1994
Developed	90	91	100	100	102	104	104
Developing	125	109	100	98	99	100	96
India	65	92	100	91	114	NA	NA

7. Developing economies, with exports dominated by primary products, lost out to developed economies. Relavtive abundance of supply of primary products as well as the superior bargaining strength of developed countries have often ben adduced as two major reasons for the deterioration in the terms of trace. Gains in the terms of trade for India in the comparable period perhaps reflects her diversified export base as well as the relatively low international prices of oil in the relevant period.

India is committed to further liberalisation of its import regime, notwithstanding the dismantling of licensing controls over a wide area. At the same time, there are concerns whether developed nations of the world are implementing in letter and spirit their part of the obligations under the Uruguay Round Agreements. Many contries are resorting to protectinist devices in the guise of environmental hazards and exploitation of labour such as child labour. The obligations of providing access to imports of developing countries, especially textiles and garments, are being circumvented under one pretext or the other, even under the back-loaded integration of Textiles and Clothing into the World Trading System. Such restrictions are designed to keep out cheaper imports.

By virtue of the radical shift from a highly-regulated to an outward-oriented economy, India has attracted immense interest abroad, at both Governmental and private investor levels. India is one of the largest emerging markets, second only to China's, and the country has been experiencing inflows of foreign portfolio and direct investments—thought not as large as in China and a few other countries—which were unthinkable in the world of even 1980s. Economic strength has become the principal determinant of a nation's standing in the international community, and even the most powerful country, the United States of America, looks for market opportunities all over, more especially in the dynamic Asia-Pacific region, as the best shield of security.

With the end of the Cold War, the East-West barriers have broken down. The rapid spread of liberalisation and globalisation is a historic development which has blurred both East-West and North-South divisions. Developing countries have been compelled to adapt themselves to conditions of global interdependence although in the process they run grave risks in the medium-term and rare not assured of international safety nets.

In the rapidly changing world environment, each developing country must certainly concentrate on building its inherent strength and developing areas of comparative advantage and forge alliances with neighbours and, where promising, enter regional blocs which offer greater opportunities of trade and other exchanges to enhance national arena, disadvantaged nations must make common cause and unite to advance their pressing needs more effectively than what has been witnessed over the last fifty years in the post-decolonisation era. This is the only way of securing a post-cold war order which is just and equitable.

India has a long way to go before it could emerge as a

strong global player, as currently it occupies the 32nd place as a leading exporter of merchandise, well below several countries in East and South-East Asia. It has to make up for the time lost in its inward-looking route to development which left the cuntry far behind in the international league, despite building a strong industrial base and possessing highly technical manpower, the third largest in the world. Indian planning did not take sufficient note of the gathering pace of global intergration with the frowth of merchandise trade exceeding the growth of output in virtually every year of the post-war period.

In recent years, India has begun to look East, is now a full dialogue partner in ASEAN (the 7-member Association of South East Nations) and excepts to find a place in the Asia Pacific Economic Forum (APEC) by 1999. These should promote greater intra-Asian trade and investment flows even as India strives to gain an increasing share of exports into developed economies of the West such as the European Union and North America. Trade with Russia and Eastern Europe as well as Central Asian States holds prospects of considerable expansion over present levels and a more promising development is the initiative taken by 14 states of the Indian Ocean Rim for an economic cooperation grouping with a Charter expected to be signed in March 1997.

The bilateral and pluralistic approaches cannot, and should not, in any way dilute India's firm commitment to multilaterialism which is the best safeguard against domination of the global economy by a few powerful nations. India's immediate responsibility is to solidify South Asian cooperation through SAPTA and ensure its early graduation to becomes SAFTA (South Asian Free Trade Area) to make it a region of good neighbourliness less prone to conflilcts than at present. With 16 per cent of the world's population, India's weight in the international economy remains negligible, and the building up of internal strength with determination through higher saving, and investments and greater efficiency in the use of resources is a pre-requisite for the country to claim its due share in the global market-place.

Growth & development of Indian consultancy

A rich blend

The Indian consultancy scenario is a rich blend of both "self-developed" technology on one hand and "acquired" know-how on the other. When the country emerged into freedom in 1947 the Indian Economy was at a low ebb with impoverished resources, processes and infrastructure designed to meet vested requirements and an environment wherein the wherewithal for nurturing and training technical and managerial talent was hardly there. The country soon took stock of the situation. National priorities were identified and a well conceived policy of "planned development" was adopted. Economic re-generation & growth forced an important segment in these planning programmes with socio-economic factors, like medicare, education, technical training, employment etc. appropriately dovetailed. It was recognised that for all these programmes or activities it was essential to nurture, encourage and develop an effective cadre of professionals, both technical and managerial. The concept of consultancy was thus ushered in and gathered strength gradually.

Self-reliance

In the course of these four score and more years-in an environment of growth and development-the Indian consultant has been sufficiently exposed not only to the technological development and consultancy practices in other countries but also is a part of the indigenous consultancy culture that has evolved as an achievement towards the national objective of self-reliance. India's commitment to self-reliance in engineering skills has ensured a fairly good growth of the consultancy sector. As a part of the overall strategy for industrial development, the utilisation of indigenous design and engineering inputs is one of the key factors. The sixties and seventies witnessed the emergence of several consultancy organisations, with specialisation in various sectors of industry. Some of these were set up in collaboration with foreign organisations while many others were set up totally with local expertise.

CDC/FIEO survey

According to a survey recently conducted by the Consultancy Development Centre (CDC) and the Federation of Indian Export Organisations (FIEO), Both non-profit institutions set up by the Government of India to service Indian Consultancy-there are more then 1400 consultancy organisations and individual consultants (both management and technical) rendering services in various aspects of industrial and non-industrial sectors of the economy.

Trend of growth

The trend of growth of consultancy during the periods 1940-1988 is shown in the Table below:

Growth trend of Indian consultancy

Period	*Annual Growth %*
1940 – 60	5
1961 – 80	43
1981 – 88	52

Growth indicators

During the course of the last 5 years the number of consultancy firms in the country has country has increased from 700 to 1400; the consultancy turnover from Rs. 500 to Rs. 1000 crores; employment in the consultancy profession from 40,000 to 80,000 and exports of consultancy services from Rs. 50 to Rs. 120 crores.

Nascent stage

In spite of this growth, and keeping in mind that the consultancy culture has assumed some dimensions in India's national economic infrastructure only recently, Indian consultancy, in spite of its achievements, is yet in its nascent stage.

Entrepreneurship development

The three decades of continues growth have brought maturity to the movement of entrepreneurship development in India. Till the beginning of the 1960s, entrepreneurship remained a topic of academic and philosophical discussion by economist, sociologist and psychologist. The attempt was to accurately define and describe entrepreneurship, its nature and functions. Such description were markedly influenced by respective academic disciplines. Although most of these descriptions were partly true, yet none of them had the quality of describing entrepreneurship as a whole. Towards the end of the 60s, two very significant contributions were made in the field of entrepreneurship. These were:

(i) Establishment of positive linkages between entrepreneurship and economic prosperity. 1 and

(ii) Emergence of strong hypothese that entrepreneurship can be developed through planned efforts.

The former helped acceptance of entrepreneurship development for achieving economic prosperity and the later facilitated experimentation with various strategies for developing entrepreneurship.

In 70's varieties of strategies and models of developing entrepreneurship were developed, repeated and replicated. As a result entrepreneurship was identified as important vehicle of industrial development which is evident by the emergence of about 1.7 million SSI enterprises creating jobs for more than 10 million workers in the sector. During 80's the structure and functions needed for promoting entrepreneurship become more or less clear and entrepreneurship attained the status of a movement. At national level during 1982-83 National Science & Entrepreneurship Development Board (NSEDB) and National Entrepreneurship Development Board (NEDB) were created under the Chairmanship of the Prime Minister and Union Minister for Industry respectively. Two national resource institutions, i.e., National Institute for Entrepreneurship & Small Business Development (NIESBUD) at New Delhi and Entrepreneurship development Institute of India (EDII) at Ahmedabad were established during the same period. Presently more than 700 organisations including 7 state level entrepreneurship development institutes, 27 SISIs under SIDO, 17 TCOs, 20 Engineering and Technical Institution, 7 STEOs and a host of non-governmental organisations are engaged in developing entrepreneurship. SIDO alone has trained more than 50,000 potential entrepreneurs during 78-88 and one Centre for Entrepreneurship Development of Gujarat trained more than 10,000 potential entrepreneurs since its inception. In this way thousand of people get opportunities to be developed as entrepreneurs. But the coverage is still far less as compared to the potential available in the country. We may have to took into the infrastructural facility, availability and accessibility to information and technology and develop enormously large cader of trainers and poromoters to reach both urban and rural population. To illustrate, during the 8th Five Year Plan, as per the modest calculations, the country needs about 13,000 trainers, promoters for training potential entrepreneurs as against few hundred which are available today.

The mid 70s witnessed the crystallisation of an integrated model for Entrepreneurship Decelopment (EDP), consisting of *stimulatory, support* and *sustaining activities*. This was replicated and very widely with minor variations. The present decade is shaping up to be *"age of entrepreneurial explosion"*. It is visiable as a significant programme in national development plan. During 80s, the structure and function needed for promoting entrepreneurship have become more or less clear. With growing emphasis by the Government and the matching enthusiasm by NGOs, entrepreneurship has now attained the status of a movement.

The movement of entrepreneurship development in India, however, started as part of the total strategy of small industry development. The dynamic SSI policy has strongly supported the cause of entrepreneurship development and both have mutually supplemented each other.

Presently, Small Scale Industries in India are defined by investment limit of Rs. 6 million (Rs. 7.5 million for ancillary units). Besides manufacturing, services, maintenance and processing enterprises are also included in SSI. The tiny sector which has been given the distinctive position is defined as consisting of those units having investment less than Rs. 0.5 million.

The response to such dynamic policy has been very rewarding. The growth of SSI Sector has been one of the most impressive. Between 1973-74 and 1986-87 the number of SSI increased by over 3 folds from 0.416 million to nearly 1.457 million. Presently (1990) their number is estimated as 1.7 million. Employment in this sector has risen more than double from nearly 3.47 million to 10.14 million. The value of Production in terms of current prices increased ten times (Rs. 72,000 million to Rs. 722,500 million). In the field of export, SSI conribution was recorded as approximately 30 per cent of the country's total exports.

More impressive than these statistics is the number crossing 5,000 products which are manufactured in the small scale sector. Beginning with the production of simple consumer goods, the small scale today manufacturs several sophisticated, precision items using latest technology. Some of the sophisticated items precision items using latest technology. Some of the sophisticated items produced in SSI sector include T.V., electronic disk calculator, micro-wave components, electro-medical equipment, miniature bulbs, optical lens, digital measuring equipments, air-conditioning equipments, electric motors, machine tools, authomobile and scooter parts.

Small enterprises in India were also found more economical than large enterprises in terms of capital investment and development generation. Further, small enterprises are providing learning ground for imparting, managerial, entrepreneurial and technical skills. They also provide an outlet for creative urge among individuals to persue excellence in product design and innovations resulting into competitive culture and problem solving orientation which usually lack at the initial stage of development but are basic to socio-economic prosperity. The most significant aspect of small industry development is that this sector has stimulated vigorously the economic activity of a far reaching magnitude and created a sense of confidence among very large number of small entrepreneurs about their strength and vitality.

FERA being replaced

In keeping with the cuntry's progress towards a more

open economy with greater trade and investment linkages with the rest of the world, Mr. Chidambaram said he would introduce later in the year a new Act to replace the Foreign Exchange Regulation Act. 1973 (FERA). At the same time, he signalled a move toward convertibility of the rupee on capital account with his decision to ask the Reserve Bank to set up an expert group to lay out the road map and work out a time table for achieving the goal. A beginning in agricultural sector reform has also been made with the decision to repeal regulations governing rice milling and ginning and pressing factories. Domestic future trading is to be resumed in ginned and baled cotton, raw jute and jute goods.

In formulating his tax proposals, Mr. Chidambaram set himself a target of increasing the net tax revenues of the Centre by 15 to 16 per cent in 1997—98. Notwithstanding the rate reductions and reliefs he has extended, the Finance Minister hopes to make up the loss by better collections. For the corporate sector, he has not only reduced the tax rate to 35 per cent but also abolished the tax on dividends in the hands of the share holder. He, however, proposed a 10 per cent tax on profits distributed in order to persuade companies to invest them for future growth.

Mr. Chidambaram rejected the demand for withdrawal of the controversial Minimum Alternate Tax (MAT) he introduced last year but announced exemption of export profits from MAT. He has also revised the manner in which MAT is charged and collected with a provision for tax credit. He has accepted the Corporate Sector's demand for buy—back of shares by companies and said an overall ceiling of 60 per cent will be kept for intercorporate investment and loans. Another proposal to boost the capital market is a one—time permission to stock brokers to corporatise their business without attracting tax on capital gains which will be exempted.

Tariff reforms

After an interval of one year, Mr. Chidambaram has taken up tariff reform reducing the peak rate of customs duty from 50 to 40 per cent. In the process, he reduced import duty on products which are inputs of the steel industry like coking coal, or on items which would help industries like engineering, textiles, chemicals and host of items related to information technology. The Power sector will get relief with the cut in the duty on non—coking coal from 20 to 10 per cent. In excise duty, Mr. Chidambaram has sought to simplify the structure with three new rates of 8, 13 and 18 per cent, rationalising the existing rates in the process.

The only tax measure in the budget is a tax on certain services calculated to yield Rs. 900 crore in 1997—98 and Rs. 1200 crore in a full year. The net gain to the Centre will however, be only Rs. 300 crore because of the lowering of the interest tax on banks, which would result in a loss of revenue of Rs. 600 crore.

Despite the burdens thrown by the Fifth Pay Commission recommendations, higher provisions for subsidies, defence and interest payments, Mr. Chidambaram has managed to bring about a reduction in revenue deficit from 2.3 per cent of G.D.P. in the current year to 2.1 per cent next year. He has also increased the budget support for the Central Plan outlay by Rs. 6000 crore.

Mr. Chidambaram has framed his budget against the background of an economy which has been growing at an average rate of 7 per cent during the last three years. He is confident that GDP growth will be sustained at this level or even improved upon in the coming year, though he has listed some areas of concern. These are the sharp decline in crude oil production, poor performance of power sector, the slowdown in export growth, rise in the rate of inflation and volatile capital market. He asserts that his budget proposals are aimed at addressing these concerns. To maintain price stability, he has expressed his determination to adhere toa prudent fiscal policy, contain growth of money supply within 16 per cent and resort to liberal imports of wheat and other essential commodities to counter the pressure on prices. The coming months would show how far the Finance Minister's expectations including price stability (are) are fulfilled. He has indeed given a kick start to an economy which had been widely perceived to have begun to falter in recent months.

Application for collaboration approval

All foreign investment proposals and technical license agreements require approval from either the Secretariat of Industrial Approval (SIA) or the Reserve Bank of Inida (RBI) depending on the applicable criteria.

Applications for approval of technical collaborations requiring clearance by Reserve Bank should henceforth be made in form FC(RBI) (10 copies) to the Controller Exchange Control Department, Foreign Investment and Technology Transfer Section, Reserve Bank of India, Central Office, Bombay -400 023. Applications requiring clearance of the Government of India should be submitted in form FC(SIA) (10 copies) to the Entrepreneurial Assistance Unit of the Secretariat for Industrial Approvals (SIA) in the Department of Industrial Development, Ministry of Industry, Government of India, Udyog Bhawan, New Delhi - 110 011. Copies of both the Forms along with the guidelines issued by the Reserve Bank of India have been annexed ot this Update so as to assist the reader in knowing the type of information that would have to be supplied to the Indian Authorities.

Following the statement that permission to bring in technology and/or equity participation has been made 'automatic', several notifications and clarifications have been announced by the Government and by Reserve Bank of India regarding the procedural requirements prior to securing such permission. These announcements and policy changes continue to be announced on a day to day basis. Before advising a client or embarking upon a new foreign investment related project, it may therefore be appropriate to seek professional advice and assistance.

Foreign investment promotion board

A specially empowered board namely the Foreign Investment Promotion Board (FIPB) has been constituted and has been vested with enough flexibility to examine those offers that do not come under the purviews of either the RBI or the SIA on a case by case basis. This board, located in the office of the Prime Minister has as its Chairman the Principal Secretary to the Prime Minister. The objective of the Board is to invite and facilitate investment in India by international companies in projects which are considered to be of benefit to the Indian economy and do not fall within the parameters of the existing policy for clearance of foreign investment proposals. The Board will provide a single window clearance for all aspects of projects considered by it.

The Investment Week issue of November 16, 1992 reports that the Foreign Investment Promotion Board has recently cleared 23 more foreign Investment proposals, most of which are 100% Export Oriented Units, (EOUS) and in the small scale sector.

The investment proposals to the FIPB can be in the form of a plain letter, without any prescribed format and will be decided on the basis of the relevant details given. According to the Government's statement in the Lok Sabha on 15th July, 1992 the criteria for clearing these cases are export potential, employment potential and other benefits likely to accure from the projects. It has been reported that almost all the cases submitted to the SIA and the FIPB in the last few months have received the necessary approvals expeditiously.

Automatic Approval of Foreign Investment and Technology Transfer

The FITT section was set up in the Central Office of the Exchange Control Department at Bombay on 16th September, 1991.

Till 26th September 1992 the FITT had received 996 applications of which 733 were approved and 221 returned for want of certain prerequisites and stipulated conditions being fulfilled by applicants.

The bulk of foreign investments approved were in the chemicals industry, electricals/electronics, food processing, industrial machinery and scientific and electrical laboratory equipment.

Cabinet Committee on Foreign Investment (CCFI)

Proposals involving equity investment over Rs. 3000/- million are submitted to and approved by the CCFI which is headed by the Prime Minister.

A new liberalised policy pakage for the garments sector has been approved at a meeting of the CCFI. The new policy will also enable the garments sector unit to raise its capacity through technologies upgradation and increase investment upto Rs. 30 million provided it exports half of its production.

Opening of branch offices in India

The Reserve bank of India in January, 1992 liberalised the branch licensing policy for foreign banks after nearly two decades. Foreign banks have sought 44 more branches as a result.

Foreign companies engaged in the manufacturing and trading activities abroad are now permitted to open branch offices in India for carrying on certain activities as follows:

— to represent the parent company/other foreign companies in various matters in India eg. as buying/selling agents in India etc;

— to conduct research work in which the parent company is engaged provided the results of the research are made available to the Indian companies;

— to undertake export and import trading activities;

— to promote possible technical & financial collaborations between the Indian companies & overseas companies.

Industry wise update

A brief industry wise Update of the changes in some key industries is given below:

Electronics/computers: software

The Government of India has recently notified the electronic hardware technology park (EHTP) scheme for building a strong electronics industry with emphasis on enhancing its export potential. For this purpose, foreign equity upto 100% has been allowed in the case of such units. Such a park can be set up by the Central Government, State Governments and public or privates sector organisations. Multinational companies, setting up manufacturing facilities in computer hardware and peripherals under 100% EOU Scheme will be allowed to sell upto 30% of their production in the domestic market. These companies will be allowed to import, paying upto a maximum of 30% import duty, raw materials, plant and machinery.

The following are the recently announced procedural measures initiated by the Government for the delicensing and decentralising of the Electronics Sector:

— The entire electronic industry has been exempted from the locational limitations imposed on other industries and may thus be located even in urban areas.

— Licensing has been abolished for all industrial undertakings including companies covered under Monopolies and Restrictive Trade Practices (MRTP) and Foreign Exchange Regulation Act (FERA) except the sub-sector of consumer electronics and strategic electronics.

— The system of phased manufacturing programme (PMP) run on case by case basis has been abolished.

— Development of small scale industries is being encouraged. Approvals/registrations have been totally decentralised to the level of State Directorates of Industries.

— Existing units are permitted to manufacture any article without additional investment under broad-banding subject to certain conditions.

— As recently as 20th November, 1992 the Commerce Ministry has by a notification significantly liberalised the advance licensing scheme for the electronics sector. The Government has substantially reduced and rationalised the value addition norms as well as input output norms for various electronic items, particularly components, with a view to boosting electronic exports from the country.

Software

As India tries to integrate with the world economy some major changes affecting the Indian Software Industry have been initiated by the Government of India.

— Software industry is a 'high priority industry', thus it qualifies for automatic approval by the RBI for 'foreign technology agreements'.

— In March 1992, the Indian Department of Electronics (DOE) authorised the reproduction of foreign software for distribution within India if the local distribution fulfils certain conditions.

— The new Import-Export Policy has substantially eliminated import licensing, quantitative restrictions and other regulatory and discriminatory controls on the import of software.

Tax benefits for the software industry

In order to boost Software exports, the Government of India in the Union Budget 1991-92 has provided a new section whereby an assessee engaged in the business of export of computer software or rendering of technical software services outside India is allowed a pro-rata deduction for the next 3 assessment years. The pro-rata deduction is computed on a formula which takes into consideration the percentage of revenue earned from the export division. If the total income of a software business is generated from exports only, 100% exemption from income tax would be available. This exemption supplements the deduction available in respect of export profits under section 80 HHC of the Income Tax Act 1961.

India's interest in setting up joint ventures abroad

The Government of India has consistently been in favour of establishing maintaining and steadily improving economic and technical cooperation among the developing countries and has been adopting all necessary measures for achieving these objectives, duly participating in, and promoting, the global developments of extending the frontiers of international trade and investment.

The problems in industrial development initially faced by India were similar to those faced by most other developing nations, namely, scarcity of capital, low productivity, slow rate of economic growth, absence of infrastructural facilitiess, a rapidly expending population, unemployment, inflation and other socio-economic problems. India has already achieved a considerable measure of success in resolving these during the preceding four decades or so (since the country attained independence) and is tackling the residuary problems with its sagacious economic and industrial policies, modifying in inproving them from time to time, to suit the emerging requirements of the changing times. These resilient and dynamic policies have been aimed at achieving a rapid and orderly industrialisation of the country and a steady improvement in the standard of living of its people. From self-reliance to exporting goods and services India has treaded a long path.

India's achievements on the industrial front by following such policies have been impressive. Besides increase in the volume of industrial output, there has been substantial change in the composition of industrial production over the years. India now produces machinery for textiles, sugar, cement, jute, paper etc. Apart from these, large quantities of metallurgical and heavy equipment and mining machinery are also produced. India has also gone into production of heavy electrical equipment such as power turbines and generators. Substantial capacities have been set up for the production of electric motors of different kinds, as also of various types of machine tools including high-speed lathes, milling machines, radial drills, grinding machines etc. A variety of scientific instruments are also produced.

Top priority accorded to the development of infrastructural facilities over the years has resulted in the establishment of an efficient transportatin and communication network. India has a excellent railway system, which ranks third in the world in terms of route length as well as passenger and goods traffic. There is also a very good network of roads which connects most of the villages and towns. Moreover, the communication system is well-developed and India is connected with most other countries, especially the commercial centres of the world, by modern means of communication.

There has also been tremendous growth in the financial infrastructure. Commercial banking and financial markets, especially in industrial finance, have expanded at very fast rate.

India is in aposition to offer appropriate technologies to other developing countries which are cost-effective, suited to local conditions, make maximum use of local inputs and provide maximum employment to local persons through labour orientation. Some well-known examples are the export of technology for the manufacture of trucks, three wheelers and two wheelers and pulp and paper plants.

According to reliable estimates, more than one thousand consultancy firms, besides individual professionals, are offering their services in various fields. The services offered range from preparation of market surveys, feasibility reports etc. to basic and detailed engineering services, erection and commissioning of plants, training of personnel etc.

The Indian Consultancy Organisations are today offering their services in divergent fields like engineering industries, electronic industries, ferrous and non-ferrous metallurgical industries, chemical industries, aluminium, pulp and paper, forest-based industries, mining and allied industries, urban development, sewage disposal and effluent treatment, distillation and refinery plants, chemical plants, drugs and pharmaceuticals, generation, transmission and distribution of power, railways, highways and bridges, water supply and town planning architecture and irrigation and flood control management.

The Indian enterprises have acquired necessary capabilities of offering project export services ranging from civil and construction projects to industrial projects. The scope of services varies from sub-contracting to execution of turnkey projects. In the industrial sector, the project exports from India range from low level technology areas like structural engineering and power distribution to sophisticated technology areas such as power generation, setting up of chemical plants, cement plants, transportation and tele-communication. In addition to securing a number of project contracts from the countries of West Asia, South Asia, Africa etc., the Indian industry has been able to obtain contracts for projects funded by the World Bank, the Asian Development Bank. The African Development Bank etc. in a process of competitive bidding.

Specialised services from the Indian Consultancy Organisations are available in the fields of Agriculture and Natural Resources, Energy, Oil and Gas Industry, Management Building, Public Health Engineering and Water Supply and Transport. The specific areas in which India can offer joint ventures is illustrated in Annexure I.

The Indian technology suppliers have to comply with rigorous requirements regafding import of technology, local content etc. They are thus in an advantageous position to understand the requirements and conditions of other developing countries and to adapt themselves to those conditins. The technologies offered by India will also be suited to the economies of scale of other developing countries, in addition to being of low cost. India is now in a position to export technology and services in the aforesaid areas and have many joint ventures not only in the developing but even in the highly industrialised countries.

As on 30th June, 1991 there are 159 Indian Joint Ventures in operation in 42 countries. Out of this 22 are in Europe, 7 in the United States of America, 56 in South East Asia, 24 in South Asia, 17 in West Asia, 29 in Africa and 4 in the Oceania region. Another 65 joint ventures are under various stages of implementation in these countries. Indian joint Ventures are in operation in the following areas.

(a) Engineering industries

1. Light Engineering
2. Commercial Vehicles

(b) Metallurgical industries

3. Iron and Steel Products

(c) Chemical industries

4. Textiles and Allied Products
5. Chemicals and Pharmaceuticals
6. Oil Seed Crushing and Palm Oil Refining
7. Food Products (including soft drinks)
8. Pulp and paer
9. Glass and Glass Products
10. Leather and Rubber Products
11. Cement Products

(d) Other Manufacturing Industries

(e) Service Sector

12. Hotels and Restaurants
13. Consultancy
14. Engineering contracts and construction
15. Trading and Marketing

(f) Other non-manufacturing ventures

An illustrative list of areas where India is capable of offering technologies and setting up joint ventures is given below:

Metallurgical industries

— Iron and Steel Castings

— Steel Forgings

— Rolling Mill Rolls

— Steel Rolling Mills

— Steel Wires

— Non-ferrous castings

— Aluminium Extrusion

Industrial machinery

— Rice Mill Machinery

— Sugar Mill Machinery

— Boilers

— Air and Water Pollution Control Equipment

— Power Driven Pumps

— Speed Reduction Units

— Chemical and Pharmaceutical Machinery

— Food Processing Machinery

— Pulp and Paper Making Machinery

— Power Plant Equipment

— Miscellaneous Industrial Machinery

Electrical equipment

— Electric Motors

— Alternators

— Transformers

— Condenser Bushings/Circuit Breakers/Power Capacitors

— Arc Furnaces and Induction Furnaces

— Voltage Regulators

— Electric Fans

— Household Electric Appliances

— Electric Bulbs

— Cables and Conductors

Electronic equipment

— Radios, Tape Recorders, "Two-in-Ones"

— Television Receivers

— Components like Resistors, Capacitors, Transistors and Diodes

— Printed Circuit Boards

— Micro/Mini-Computers

— Computer Software

Transportation

— Trucks, Four Wheelers, Three Wheelers, Two Wheelers, Mopeds

— Automobile Ancillaries

— Diesel Engines

— Crawler Tractors/Dumpers/Loaders

— Bicycles and Bicycle Parts

Agricultural machinery

— Agricultural Tractors and Tillers/Agricultural Implements

Machine tools

— Lathes

— Drilling Machines

— Milling Machines

— Planning Machines

— Wood Working Machinery

— Machine Tools Accessories

— Small Tools/Hand Tools

Mechanical engineering

— Structural Fabrication

— Transmission Line Towers

— Pipes and Tubes

— Typewriters

— Cash Registers

— Sewing Machines

— Bolts/Nuts/Screws/Studs

— Drums and Barrels

— Tin Containers

— Cutlery

— Pressure Cookers

— Aluminium and Steel Furniture/Office Equipment

— Steel Almirahs/Vaults/Safes

— Stoves

Other engineering industries

— Air Conditioners and Refrigerators

— Solar Water Heaters/Solar Cookers

— Mathematical and Survey Instruments

— Energy Meters/Water Meters

Chemical industry

— Bricks and Tiles

— Cement

— RCC/PCC Pipes, Poles and Sleepers

— Glass Containers

— Potassium Chlorate/Sodium Chlorate

— Fertilisers

— Carbon Black

— Aromatics and Laboratory Chemicals

— Fine Chemical and Flavours

— Cosmetics

— Soaps and Detergents

— Drugs and Pharmaceuticals

— Dye Stuffs and Dye Intermediates

— Food Processing

— Distilleries

— Soft Drink Bottling Plants

— Vegetable Oil Processing

— Solvent Extraction

— Crockery
— Ceramic Tiles
— Sanitary Wares
— Leather and Leather Products
— Paper, Pulp and Paper Products
— Paints/Enamels/Varnishes
— Rubber Products including Automobile Tyre and Tubes
— Plastic Products
— Viscose Staple Fibre
— Jute Goods
— Textiles/Yarns (Cotton/Blended/Synthetic)
— Readymade Garments
— Wooden Furniture
— Sports Goods
— Stationery Items

Environmental options for the 21st century

Human activities have pushed our planet to the brink of disaster necessitating a comprehensive global action to retrieve the situation. While explcring newer forms of renewable sources of energy to address the environmental malady, our planners and administrators need to address the most urgent task of improving energy efficiency. The rural areas should depend on minihydel projects and bioenergy as far as possible. A serious and lasting government commitment to the development and use of energy efficient and renewable technologies is the need of the hour.

Like it or not, we find ourselves in a world where we are responsible for each other's well-being. In the last few years of this millennium, difficult questions of social equality, national sovereignty, and individual rights and responsibilities are emerging. A person may be able to afford a large, energy-consumptive automobile, but can the planet afford it? Indeed, the larger question boils down as to how many carbon-emitting automobilies can the planet tolerate without the habitability of the earth being disturbed. At a more mundane level, a couple may desire and be able to support several children, but can the planet afford several children per family? Does our generation have the right to extinguish plant and animal species that have evolved over millions of years? Do we not have the obligation to preserve our biological heritage for our future generations?

An affirmative answer to these questions depends on restoring and prserving the conditions that make the earth habitable, a place capable of supporting a diversity of life and modern civilization. Human activities have pushed the planet to the brink of disaster.

Agenda for action

A comprehensive global action plan to remedy the situation should include: developing energy strategies that have climate protection as their cornerstone; expanding the earth's forest cover so as to prevent global warming; doubling the per capita grain production and lastly, breaking the momentum of population growth.

While these are the macro-level targets for making this globe a sustainable one in the forthcoming century, at the micro-level it amounts to a severe test on the capacity of world leaders as well as the local ones in their efforts in ecological economic betterment of the populations under their jurisdiction.